ADAM AND EVE AND THE GREAT RESET

Adam and Eve and the Great Reset

Jonathan Pike

Contents

Introduction - The Book They Tried to Bury   1

   Part 1 - The Declassified Pages   9

The Next Cataclysm   10

The Great Floods   15

The Story   24

The Event - 11,500 Years Ago   31

The Book of Genesis - 1,2,3   36

Conclusion   43

The Author   46

Ancient Myths – The Echo of Forgotten Worlds   48

   Part 2: What We Know Now   55

Introduction to Part 2   56

Randall Carlson – The Keeper of the Patterns   62

The Younger Dryas Smoking Gun   70

Graham Hancock – The Historian of Forgotten Worlds   76

Göbekli Tepe – The Message in Stone   79

The Boneyards of the North   88

Ben Davidson – The Solar Killshot   91

The Ethical Skeptic - ECDO Theory   95

Conclusion — The Forgotten Pattern   100

Bibliography and References

Introduction - The Book They Tried to Bury

In 1963, a small, unassuming book slipped into print under the name The Adam and Eve Story. It did not make the bestseller lists. It didn't get reviewed in the New York Times. It wasn't splashed across television talk shows. It was, in a sense, a quiet release — and yet within three years it would be taken off the table entirely. By 1966, the Central Intelligence Agency had classified it. No public explanation, no press release, no public debate. It was simply pulled out of circulation, absorbed into the great locked vault of things "not for you to see."

If it had been nonsense, it would have died of its own weight. You don't classify fairy tales. You don't treat a harmless piece of speculative fiction as if it contains weapons-grade information. Yet this one, they did. For decades, it stayed that way, until a much later "sanitized" version emerged from CIA archives — a fifty-seven-page skeleton of whatever it once was, stripped of large portions and presented as a harmless curiosity from the past.

What survives is interesting enough: a catastrophic theory of Earth's history, rooted in the idea that the planet's crust can shift catastrophically, almost overnight, wrenching entire continents into new latitudes. The poles relocate, oceans slosh over the land, mountains sink, deserts freeze, and ice caps melt into roaring inland seas. Civilizations

1

are erased not in centuries but in days. Life is reduced to scattered survivors clinging to whatever high ground remains.

This was not the slow tectonic drift you were taught in school. It was sudden, violent, global.

The man behind the book, Chan Thomas, was not just a hobbyist. He had an intelligence background himself, and there were whispers that some of what he wrote had roots in briefings or conversations far outside the public's normal reach. His narrative wasn't the first time such ideas had been aired, but the combination of scientific plausibility, historical correlation, and a chillingly detailed scenario of the next event made it stand out. Enough, apparently, to catch the attention of people whose job it is to know about such things — and to hide them. Thomas was influenced heavily by the work of Charles Hapgood, the history professor who took "Earth Crust Displacement" from fringe speculation to a theory serious enough to be commented on — even encouraged — by Albert Einstein. Hapgood had spent years examining the maps, the ice cores, the magnetic data, and even the peculiar archaeological clues scattered across the high latitudes. He was not afraid, early on, to suggest that such shifts might happen far faster than the public imagined. In his correspondence and early lectures, there are hints of a far more abrupt catastrophe — something that could unfold not in thousands of years but in a matter of months or even days.

Hapgood's own expeditions to the far north were not just academic exercises. He was mapping ancient shorelines buried under ice, looking for signs that entire climatic zones had been yanked from temperate to polar positions in a geological instant. There were mammoth carcasses with undigested summer vegetation still in their stomachs. There were forests buried under permafrost. There were ice flow patterns inconsistent with the current pole positions. His early thinking fit the old legends: a world overturned, lands drowned, the sun rising in the wrong place.

And yet, by the time his most widely read books were in print, the timelines had stretched. The sharp edges of "instant" had been rounded into something more gradual. Decades rather than days. A movement of degrees per year rather than degrees per hour. Was this the natural evolution of his thinking as he considered more evidence? Or was it something else — a quiet trimming of the sails under the pressure of institutions that preferred the public to be unalarmed? We can't say for certain. We do know that Thomas, years later, was putting the sudden shift squarely back on the table, and that when he did, his work disappeared into classified vaults.

This is the first element of the controversy: two men, overlapping in their research, one publicly softening the theory, the other having his strongest version buried. The second element is even more telling: the pattern matches exactly how sensitive knowledge is handled. First, an idea emerges. Then it gains some traction, sometimes even inside government or military channels. At a certain point, it crosses an invisible line — perhaps because new data lines up too well, perhaps because it dovetails with internal risk assessments. From that moment on, the public narrative is altered, delayed, or derailed entirely. The work is taken out of open circulation. And while the public version is diluted, the core knowledge doesn't vanish. It moves behind closed doors, into continuity-of-government planning, deep-bore shelters, and the kind of "future risk" files that never see the light of day.

If you follow the threads, you see other patterns from the same era. The sudden surge in deep underground military base construction. The investment in Arctic and Antarctic reconnaissance under the cover of Cold War rivalry. The quiet but persistent interest in paleoclimatology and geomagnetic studies, funded by agencies with no obvious reason to care about ice cores. You see satellite programs designed to track polar ice from space long before "climate change" was a public talking point. You see the fusion of astronomical and geological monitoring into joint defense initiatives.

It would be one thing if this were only a Cold War quirk, a relic of paranoia. But when you zoom out, the historical pattern runs far deeper. Ancient civilizations, in their myths and monuments, seem to have gone to absurd lengths to preserve records of the sky. Great stone observatories that mark the slow precession of the equinoxes over tens of thousands of years. Myths of suns that stood still, or rose in the west, or burned the earth. Flood stories not as vague metaphors but with consistent details — waves that reach mountain ranges, stars that vanish, fire from the sky, ice and wind that follow.

If Hapgood was right, and Thomas was closer to the raw truth, then those myths are not just stories. They are survival manuals, written in code, carved in stone, passed forward by the survivors of the last shift. And if that is the case, then the classification of The Adam and Eve Story is not an isolated curiosity — it is the modern echo of an ancient strategy: keep the masses ignorant, prepare the elite.

Fifty years later, we can see pieces of the picture Thomas and Hapgood only glimpsed. We have ice core data showing abrupt climate flips, magnetic field records proving rapid shifts in the poles, geological layers full of sudden extinction events. We have satellite measurements that confirm the poles are wandering faster than ever recorded. We know the magnetic shield is weakening at an accelerating pace. We know there have been times in the past when the entire crust may have moved relative to the mantle.

We also know that the narrative given to the public is still a slow one. The sudden version, the catastrophic version, lives on the fringes — in declassified scraps, in folklore, and in the whispers of people who once had clearances and now have nothing to lose. It is there in the CIA's reluctant release of this truncated text. It is there in the enduring refusal to release the missing chapters. It is there in the silence that falls whenever certain questions are asked in the wrong rooms.

May 18,1954

Mr.Charles H.Hapgood
c.o.M.G.Grand
55 West 11th Str.
New York City

Dear Mr.Hapgood:

I am sorry that the invitation of the
Institute for Advanced Study did not materialize. I was
not informed how this came about.

I have written a kind of introduction which
I enclose here. I am sending it to you in German knowing
that you have a capable person for translating it. I should
be obliged,nevertheless, if I can see the translation
before it is used.

Yours sincerely,

A. Einstein.

Albert Einstein.

The following pages reproduce, intact, the CIA's public-domain release of The Adam and Eve Story. It is not the whole book. It is a shadow of what Thomas originally published, and an even smaller shadow of what may have existed in classified form. It is offered here without alteration, as a document of its time and as a reminder that some truths are considered too dangerous to share in full.

After that, we will move into what we know now — five decades of science, archaeology, and pattern recognition that paint a clearer, and in some ways far more alarming, picture than even Thomas could. If the last civilization tried to warn us, we owe it to ourselves to listen, to read between the lines, and to decide whose cycle we intend to break: nature's, or the one where the few prepare and the many are left to drown.

FOREWORD *by Albert Einstein*

I frequently receive communications from people who wish to consult me concerning their unpublished ideas. It goes without saying that these ideas are very seldom possessed of scientific validity. The very first communication, however, that I received from Mr. Hapgood electrified me. His idea is original, of great simplicity, and—if it continues to prove itself—of great importance to everything that is related to the history of the earth's surface.

A great many empirical data indicate that at each point on the earth's surface that has been carefully studied, many climatic changes have taken place, apparently quite suddenly. This, according to Hapgood, is explicable if the virtually rigid outer crust of the earth undergoes, from time to time, extensive displacement over the viscous, plastic, possibly fluid inner layers. Such displacements may take place as the consequence of comparatively slight forces exerted on the crust, derived from the earth's momentum of rotation, which in turn will tend to alter the axis of rotation of the earth's crust.

In a polar region there is continual deposition of ice, which is not symmetrically distributed about the pole. The earth's rotation acts on these unsymmetrically deposited masses, and produces centrifugal momentum that is transmitted to the rigid crust of the earth. The constantly increasing centrifugal momentum produced in this way will, when it has reached a certain point, produce a movement of the earth's crust over the rest of the earth's body, and this will displace the polar regions toward the equator.

Without a doubt the earth's crust is strong enough not to give way proportionately as the ice is deposited. The only doubtful assumption is that the earth's crust can be moved easily enough over the inner layers.

The author has not confined himself to a simple presentation of this idea. He has also set forth, cautiously and comprehensively, the extraordinarily rich material that supports his displacement theory. I think that this rather astonishing, even fascinating, idea deserves the serious attention of anyone who concerns himself with the theory of the earth's development.

To close with an observation that has occurred to me while writing these lines: If the earth's crust is really so easily displaced over its substratum as this theory requires, then the rigid masses near the earth's surface must be distributed in such a way that they give rise to no other considerable centrifugal momentum, which would tend to displace the crust by centrifugal effect. I think that this deduction might be capable of verification, at least approximately. This centrifugal momentum should in any case be smaller than that produced by the masses of deposited ice.

Part 1 - The Declassified Pages

The Next Cataclysm

Like Noah's,
6,500 years ago . . . .

Like Adam and Eve's, 11,500 years ago . . . .

This, too,
will come to pass . . . .

With a rumble so low as to be inaudible, growing, throbbing, then fuming into a thundering roar, the earthquake starts.   only it's not like any earthquake
in recorded history.
In California the mountains shake like ferns in a breeze; the mighty Pacific rears back and piles up into a mountain of water more than two miles high, then starts its race eastward.
With the force of a thousand armies the wind attacks, ripping, shredding everything in its supersonic bombardment. The unbelievable mountain of Pacific sea-water follows the wind eastward, burying Los Angeles and San Francisco as if they were but grains of sand. Nothing — but nothing — stops the relentless, overwhelming onslaught of wind and ocean.
Across the continent the thousand mile-per-hour wind wreaks its unholy vengeance, everywhere, mercilessly, unceasingly. Every living thing is ripped into shreds while being blown across the countryside; and the earthquake leaves no place untouched. In many places the earth's molten sub-layer breaks through and spreads a sea of white-hot liquid fire to add to the holocaust.
Within three hours the fantastic wall of water moves across the continent, burying the wind-ravaged land under two miles of seething water coast-to-coast. In a fraction of a day all vestiges of civilization are gone, and the great cities — Los Angeles, San Francisco, Chicago, Dallas, New York — are nothing but legends. Barely a stone is left where millions walked just a few hours before.
A few lucky ones who manage to find shelter from the screaming wind on the lee side of Pike's Peak watch the sea of molten fire break through the quaking valleys below. The raging waters follow, piling higher and higher, steaming over the molten earth-fire, and rising almost to their feet. Only great mountains such as this one can withstand the cataclysmic onslaught.
North America is not alone in her death throes.
Central America suffers the same cannonade — wind, earth-fire, and

inundation.

South America finds the Andes not high enough to stop the cata-clysmic violence pounded out by nature in her berserk rage. In less than a day, Ecuador, Peru, and western Brazil are shaken madly by the devastating earthquake, burned by molten earth-fire, buried un-der cubic miles of torrential Pacific seas, and then turned into a frozen hell. Everything freezes. Man, beast, plant, and mud are all rock-hard in less than four hours.

Europe cannot escape the onslaught. The raging Atlantic piles higher and higher upon itself, following the screeching wind eastward. The Alps, Pyrenees, Urals, and Scandinavian mountains are shaken and heaved even higher before the wall of water strikes.

Western Africa and the sands of the Sahara vanish in nature's wrath, under savage attack by wind and ocean. The area bounded by the Congo, South Africa, and Kenya suffers only severe earthquakes and winds - no inundation. Survivors there marvel at the Sun, standing still in the sky for nearly half a day.

Eastern Siberia and the Orient suffer a strange fate indeed — as though a giant subterranean scythe sweeps away the earth's founda-tions, accompanied by the wind in its screaming symphony of super-sonic death and destruction. As the Arctic basin leaves its polar home, eastern Siberia, Manchuria, China, and Burma are subjected to the same annihilation as South America: wind, earth-fire, inunda-tion, and freezing. Jungle animals are shredded to ribbons by the wind, piled into mountains of flesh and bone, and buried under avalanches of seawater and mud. Then comes the terrible, paralyzing cold. Not man, nor beast, nor plant, nor earth is left unfrozen in the entire eastern Asian continent, most of which remains below sea level.

East of the Urals, in western Siberia, a few lucky people survive the fantastic winds and quakes.

Antarctica and Greenland, with their ice caps, now rotate around the earth in the Torrid Zone; and the fury of wind and inundation marches on for six days and nights. During the sixth day the oceans start to settle in their new homes, running off the high grounds. On the seventh day the horrendous rampage is over.

The Arctic ice age is ended — and a new stone age begins. The oceans — the great homogenizers — have laid down another deep layer of mud over the existing strata in the great plains, as exposed in the Grand Canyon, Painted Desert, and Badlands.

The Bay of Bengal basin, just east of India, is now at the North Pole. The Pacific Ocean, just west of Peru, is at the South Pole. Greenland and Antarctica, now rotating equatorially in the Torrid Zone, find their ice caps dissolving madly in the tropical heat. Massive walls of water and ice surge toward the oceans, taking everything — from mountains to plains — in gushing, heaving paths, creating immense seasonal moraines. In less than twenty-five years the ice caps are gone, and the oceans around the world rise over two hundred feet with the new-found water. The Torrid Zone will be shrouded in a fog for generations from the enormous amounts of moisture poured into the atmosphere by the melting ice caps.

New ice caps begin to form in the new polar areas. Greenland and Antarctica emerge with verdant, tropical foliage. Australia is the new, unexplored continent in the North Temperate Zone, with only a few handfuls of survivors populating its vastness. New York lies at the bottom of the Atlantic, shattered, melted by earth-fire, and covered by unbelievable amounts of mud. Of San Francisco and Los Angeles, not a trace is left.

Egypt emerges from its Mediterranean inundation new and higher — still the land of the ages. The commonplace of our time becomes the mysterious Baalbek of the new era.

A new era! Yes, the cataclysm has done its work well. The greatest population regulator of all does once more for man what he refuses to do for himself, and drives the pitiful few who survive into a new stone age.

Once more the earth has shifted its 60-mile thick shell, with the poles moving almost to the equator in a fraction of a day. Again the atmosphere and oceans, refusing to change direction with the earth's shell, have wiped out almost all life.

After this tumble we join Noah, Adam and Eve, Atlantis, Mu, and Olympus — and Jesus joins Osiris, Ta'aroa, Zeus, and Vishnu.

The Great Floods

N oah? Adam and Eve? Vishnu? Osiris? What do they have in common? They represent eras ages apart
— and yet, somehow, they all join hands in the next cataclysm, and walk with us.

There are others who walk with us, too: men of science — long forgotten — those who first saw that these tumbles, these cataclysmic catastrophes, or "revolutions" of the earth's shell have happened before, countless times. J. Andre DeLuc in 1779 and Georges Cuvier in 1812 were the foremost. Dolomieu, the famous mineralogist, joined the consensus, as did Escher and Forel, the Swiss geologists; also J. Andre DeLuc Jr., and Von Buch. They all agreed that the cataclysms were caused by sudden revolutions of the surface of the earth.

Cuvier, in his "Theory of the Earth," first published in 1812, based his conclusions on his unparalleled correlative research in stratigraphy, comparative anatomy, and palaeontology. At that time he wrote: "Every part of the earth, every hemisphere, every continent, exhibits the same phenomenon.   There
has, therefore, been a succession of variations in the economy of organic nature   the various catastrophes
which have disturbed the strata   have given rise to
numerous shiftings of this (continental) basin.   It is
of much importance to mark, that these repeated irruptions and retreats of the sea have neither been slow nor gradual; on the contrary,

most of the catastrophes which occasioned them have been sudden; and this is especially easy to be proved, with regard to the last of these catastrophes. I agree, therefore, with MM.

DeLuc and Dolomieu, in thinking, that if anything in geology be established, it is, that the surface of our globe has undergone a great and sudden revolution, the date of which . . . cannot be much earlier than five

or six thousand years ago (also), one preceding

revolution at least had put (the continents) under water

. . . perhaps two or three irruptions of the sea."

   "These alternations now appear to me to form the problem in geology that it is of most importance to solve in order to solve it satisfactorily, it would be

necessary to discover the cause of these events. . . . These ideas have haunted, I may almost say have tormented me, during my researches among fossil bones

. . . researches which embrace but a very small part of those phenomena of the age preceding the last general revolution of the globe, and which are yet intimately connected with all the others.   "

Many attempts have been made to answer the charge made to the geological profession by Cuvier to explain these sudden revolutions. Among others, Velikovsky tried it through his study of myths and legends; Hapgood tried it; Brown attempted, and in the process amassed a tremendous library of geological data.

Every time the cataclysmic concept has come to life, the "beast" has been stoned, burned at the stake, beaten to a pulp, and buried with a vengeance; but the corpse simply won't stay dead. Each time, it raises the lid of its coffin and says in sepulchral tones: "You will die before I."

The latest of the challengers is Prof. Frank C. Hibben, who in his book,1 "The Lost Americans," said:

" This was no ordinary extinction of a vague

geological period which fizzled to an uncertain end. This death was

catastrophic and all inclusive. What
caused the death of forty million animals. The
"corpus delicti" in this mystery may be found almost anywhere.
Their bones lie bleaching in the sands of
Florida and in the gravels of New Jersey. They weather out of the dry
terraces of Texas and protrude from the sticky ooze of the tar pits off
Wilshire Boulevard in Los Angeles. The bodies of the victims are
everywhere.
... We find literally thousands together young and
old, foal with dam, calf with cow. The muck pits of
Alaska are filled with evidence of universal death a
picture of quick extinction. Any argument as to the
cause must apply to North America, Siberia, and
Europe as well.
" Mammoth and bison were torn and twisted as
though by a cosmic hand in a godly rage.
" In many places the Alaskan muck blanket is
packed with animal bones and debris in trainload lots
... mammoth, mastodon bison, horses, wolves,
bears, and lions. ... A faunal population in the
middle of some cataclysmic catastrophe was
suddenly frozen in a grim charade."
Fantastic winds; volcanic burning; inundation and burial in muck;
preservation by deep-freeze. "Any good solution to a consuming mystery must answer all of the facts," challenges Hibben.The challenge
wouldn't leave me alone. Like a hunger, it gnawed at my subcon-
scious. I could hear the deep tones of Cuvier's challenge, "find the
cause of these events," still reverberating through the sacred halls of
science, ghostly, unanswered. I felt Hibben's challenge later on, prod-
ding: ". . . answer all of the facts." I decided that this cataclysmic concept, this catastrophic end which seems to visit our planet time after
time, needed verification or refutation once and for all.
The first step was to gather all of the known, accepted data from as

many "earth" sciences as possible: stratigraphy, archaeology, anthropology, palaeontology, radiology, oceanography, seismology, glaciology, and many other fields. Correlation of the data between the sciences gave the answer: although there is enough data in each science to indicate that these cataclysms happen, there was not enough to prove the concept; but between-science correlation showed indeed that the concept was true. Not only did it verify that the events have happened, but disclosed when the last five cataclysms were, and what positions the shell of the Earth has been in for the last 35,000 years.

So, after years of research, beginning in 1949, Cuvier's challenge had an answer: Yes, indeed the cataclysms do happen. And the last one, 6,500 years ago, was Noah's Flood!

All right. So they happen; what is it that happens each time? The challenge was really two-fold: Find the process — what happens in a cataclysm; and the trigger

— what causes a cataclysm to start.

What a chase! And what a dramatic story of the earth's history we uncovered: Civilizations of 20,000 years ago more advanced than our wildest imagination; prehistoric legends from Greece, Egypt, India, and South America which became history instead of legend; lost continents in the Atlantic and Pacific which became dated realities, with logical reasons for their sudden disappearance.

Yes, Vishnu came alive: a man who lived through a cataclysm 70,000 years before our time — actually ten cataclysms ago! Now he is known as the Hindu god of ten resurrections from the waters. Osiris, too, was rediscovered; he was the Jesus of his time — a man of Egypt, some 15,000 years ago. Noah smiled at us from the pages of the "Epic of Gilgamesh"; he actually was a Sumerian named Utnapishtim, who lived 6,500 years ago. The ark he built is more than legend.

The process of a cataclysm is known now. Look at the cross-section of the Earth inside the front cover. You'll see two molten layers — the orange ones. The important one is the thin molten layer about 60 miles thick, which is between 60 and 120 miles down, below the surface of the earth. The thick, deep molten layer, starting 1800 miles down at the bottom of the mantle, and extending 1300 miles deeper, is the outer core.

Now both molten layers are liquid; however, the inner magnetic and electrical structure of the Earth makes these layers act as if they were near solid, or plastic. As long as the magnetic and electrical structure maintains its orderliness, this old earth keeps on rotating on its axis in a normal manner.

The growing ice caps — Antarctica and Greenland — are not centered on the earth's axis; and, because they rotate around the poles, are trying to swing down to the equator. The only way they could do it would be to pull the whole 60-mile thick shell around with them. As long as the shallow molten layer stays plastic, the shell won't shift; but once every few thousand years the magnetic and electrical orderliness inside the Earth is disrupted, and the molten layer is allowed to act like a free liquid, which it was all the time anyway. It then serves as a lubricant for the ice caps to pull the shell of the earth around the inside.

In ¼ to ½ a day the poles move almost to the equator, and all hell lets loose. The atmosphere and oceans don't shift with the shell — they just keep on rotating West to East — and at the equator that speed is 1000 miles per hour. It has to be, normally, to make one rotation per day. So, while the shell shifts with the poles going toward the equator, the winds and oceans go eastward, blowing across the face of the earth with supersonic speeds, inundating continents with water miles deep.

Now what about the trigger? This turned out to be the most elusive piece of the whole puzzle. We couldn't rely on some supernatural explanation — like sometime happenings in the heavens of a vague character which actually violated the laws of nature; no, it had to be something natural, a part of nature's ordinary structure, which disrupts the Earth's inner electrical and magnetic structure whenever it happens.

We once thought that Sun spots could be the cause, because they do disrupt the earth's inner electrical and magnetic structure; but we were wrong.

We found out that "nature's power plant" is a motor-generator system existing in many different magnitudes. It's a basic structure of the universe. The energy structure of an atom is identical to a rotating planet; to a blue-white star; to a galaxy; to a supergalaxy; to all levels of supergalaxies including a universe and even more. As a neutron which has escaped from its parent atom's neutral zone will separate into particles, a star — through a sunspot — gives off neutral matter which explodes as it becomes energized; so a galaxy gives birth to an exploding star when a "dead" star escapes from its neutral zone in the center; and as a "dead" galaxy explodes when it escapes from the central neutral zone of its parent supergalaxy. A planet, therefore, must act the same at its energy level.

So, apparently once every few thousand years neutral matter escapes from the 860-mile-radius inner core into the 1300-mile thick molten outer core, and there is a literal atomic explosion inside the Earth. The explosion in the high energy layer of the outer core disrupts completely the electrical and magnetic structure in both the molten outer core and the outer 60-mile thick molten layer. Finally the ice caps are allowed to pull the shell of the earth around the interior, with the shallow molten layer lubricating the shift all the way.

You can see, then, that ice ages are not a matter of advancing and retreating ice; it's simply that different areas of the Earth are in polar regions at different times, for different durations of time, with the changes between positions taking place in a fraction of a day.

The story around the world gives a silent testimony:

—The Beresovka mammoth, frozen in mud, with buttercups in his mouth;

—The age of the gorges below Niagara Falls and St.

Anthony's Falls, both about 6,500 years;

—The sudden end of the Laurentian Basin ice cap in Canada, about

11,500 years ago;

—The uninterrupted years of evolution on the Galapagos, over 11,000;

—The geological datings in the Murrumbidgee River Basin system in Australia, showing the end of an ice cap there about 11,500 years ago;

—The age of fossil bones taken from the Wilshire Boulevard tar pits, over 11,000 years;

—The sudden end of all work in the prehistoric city of Tiahuanaco, Peru, 9,550 B.C., or 11,500 years ago;

—Leonard Woolley's great work in the Holy Land, dating Noah's flood at about 6,000 years ago;

—The end of the Wisconsin ice cap, about 29,000 years ago;

—The sudden 200-foot rise of the oceans all over the world 6,000 to 7,000 years ago;

—The sudden rise of the St. Lawrence River bed 6,500 years ago;

—The changing levels of the shoreline in the Hudson Bay;

—The granite blocks from the Alps, sitting on the eastern slopes of the Jura mountains, at 4,000 feet above sea level;

—The great legendarian Fraser's uncovering of over 8,000 separate inundation survival legends in the Malay Peninsula region;

—The Pejark Marsh in Australia, which shows a quick extinction of a civilization 11,500 years ago;

—The Piri Reis map, showing the North Pole in the Sudan Basin;

—The Egyptian water-clock, showing agreement with the Piri Reis map;

—Granite on top of the mountains around Death Valley in California!

—The great stratifications of the Grand Canyon, Painted Desert, and Badlands, each layer homogenous, showing it to be deposited there suddenly by fantastic amounts of water;

—The computable age of the Antarctic and Greenland ice caps, about 6,500 years;

—The present growth of the Antarctic ice cap, about 293 cubic miles per year;

—The legends from primitive man in Tierra del Fuego at the southern tip of South America of the day the Sun set in the wrong direction;

—The legends from primitive man in Peru of the day the Sun stood still;

—The legends from Malayan and Sumatran aborigines of the long night;

—The varve (earth strata) counts in Wrenshall, Minnesota and Hackensack, New Jersey, which agree;

—The prevalence of jade in the Orient, which is material heaved up from the mantle, near equatorial pivot points during a tumble;

—The fantastic evidence of a burgeoning tropical population in Arctic Siberia and Alaska, completely wiped out in a fraction of a day;

—The similarity of languages the world over, from Polynesian to Greek, to Egyptian, to Mayan, to Eskimo, to Yakut, to Oriental, and more;

—The correlation of ice ages and quick extinctions the world over;

—The survival of primitive life at equatorial pivot points — the last two being the Malay Peninsula and the Galapagos, now rife with lizards;

—The existence of a coral reef on the floor of the Arctic Ocean;

—And more, and more, and more, and more, give us a historical picture of the Earth's shell during the past 35,000 years.

The overwhelming evidence, when put in order, gives a dramatic picture of which areas have been at the North Pole, when they moved to the pole, and how long they were there:

North Polar Eras (Areas at N. Pole)	Start (Yrs. Ago)	End (Yrs. Ago)	Duration (Yrs.)
Arctic Ocean	6,500	?	?
Sudan Basin	11,500	6,500	5,000
Hudson Bay	18,500	11,500	7,000
Caspian Sea	29,000	18,500	10,500
Wisconsin	35,000	29,000	6,000

Yes, Noah, Adam and Eve, Osiris, Ta'aroa, Zeus, and Vishnu have much deeper meanings now; and, as they join hands and walk with us, we hear Adam and Eve saying:

"Listen — for now we can truly share our story with you!"

The Story

It's funny how some things can plague you from childhood through your adult years. Not big things, but little things, which don't exactly persist, but annoyingly stick their head through your life's door and say "Boo!" just to let you know they're still there. If I made a list of all these things in my life it might take up a whole book.

I'd like to talk about just one of these bugaboos.

From the first time I heard the story of the creation and Adam and Eve, it "buzzed" me, as my young son would say. Now, to me the answer was not simply one of two usual alternatives: either unquestioning faith in the story as it stands, or complete repudiation as utter nonsense.

No, the answer seemed to lie elsewhere. If the story were taught as the truth so uniformly, in spite of its apparent divergence from scientific truths, then to me the true course would seem to be a search for the foundation of the story, which would then lead to a true reading of it. The pursuit happened almost by accident. Years of data correlation in studying the earth tumbling concept has shown the last tumble to have occurred about 6500 years ago; that Noah, or Utnapishtim, or whatever his name was, did exist and did survive that particular cataclysm.

A friend of mine suggested that Genesis I is almost a perfect description of conditions on our planet immediately following a tumble. On rereading it, I had to agree; Genesis II even mentions that a mist, or flood, went up from the earth and watered the whole face of the ground.

Well, now! This was worth thinking about. If it were so, then it would be the tumble preceding Noah's (another fascinating story!), about 11,500 years ago. This, then could be approximately the time of the Adam and Eve story.

The pursuit started. If the story did originate with that tumble, in what language was it first written?

Certainly not Hebrew or Greek, for as far as we know, they didn't exist at that time.

If we look to men such as Don Antonio Batres Juarequi and James Churchward, we may have our answer. Certainly their knowledge of prehistoric languages could be a key, and later We'll discuss the role of Naga and Ancient Mayan in the story of Adam and Eve; first, however, let's examine the history of Genesis I, II, and III.

There are many schools of thought on this subject, but the most predominant one is that Moses was the originator. This seems not too far-fetched, since Moses was reared in the Egyptian tradition, in a royal household, and probably had access to many religious writings and teachings now lost with the passing of the archives of Egypt, in Alexandria, Heliopolis, and Sais. Certainly the Ten Commandments were a condensation of the forty-two questions of Osiris for entering heaven. If Moses did write part of the Old Testament, he then must have had Naga tablet writings, or Egyptian interpretations of them, handed down to the Egyptians for thousands of years; and the Egyptian priesthood had knowledge of a cataclysm 11,500 years ago. Priests of Egypt are supposed to have told Solon during his ten years in Egypt (about 600 B.C.) that 9,000 years before that time there was a cataclysm which buried Atlantis beneath the ocean. Note that 9,000 + 600 B.C. + 1950 A.D. equals 11,5 50 years ago.

Moses' brother, Aaron, became the first chief priest of the Hebrews about 1300 B.C. Somewhere between 15 and 18 generations later, the chief priesthood having been handed down father-son through the generations, Seraiah (or Seraias) was the chief priest (See Ezra, and 1 and 2 Ezdras). In 586 B.C., in the 19th year of Nebuchadnezzar's reign, Seraiah was taken and executed, and his son Ezra made a captive in Persia (see 2 Kings). At that time, Jerusalem was sacked, and all Hebrew records including their laws and records of the Old Testament were burned with the temple at Jerusalem, by Nebuza-adan, Nebuchadnezzar's captain of the guard.

In 458 B.C., during the seventh year of Artaxerxes I's reign in Persia, Ezra was commissioned to reestablish the Hebrew religion and law. According to 2 Ezdras, Ezra rewrote the history of the Hebrews from the beginning, and reestablished their laws.

Now, from 586 to 458 B.C. is 128 years. The latest that Ezra could have been born was after his father Seraiah's murder, as well could be (see Onan's story, Genesis 38:8-10); therefore, the youngest he could have been in 458 B.C. was 127. He was working on a long memory.

Let's examine this anomaly. As mentioned before, the lineage from Aaron to Ezra contains from 17 to 20 generations, including Aaron and Ezra. Assuming (1) 1300 B.C. for the start of Aaron's priesthood (1290 B.C. is adjudged the time of the Exodus) ; (2) 458 B.C. to be near the end of Ezra's priesthood; then we find the average priesthood term per generation to be between 42.1 and 49.5 years. In view of this, can we believe that Ezra served his priesthood for approximately 130 years?

It would appear much more plausible to assume that it was Ezra's grandfather, Azariah rather than his father Seraiah, who was the one taken and executed by Nebuchadnezzar's men in 586 B.C. . Then Seraiah and Ezra would have served as chief priests during the 128 years from 586 to 458 B.C., for an average of 64 years apiece. It is even plausible that Ezra's great-grandfather Helchiah could have been the victim in 586 B.C., leaving Azariah, Seraiah, and Ezra to serve the 128 years for an average of 42 years each, which is even closer to the overall average from Aaron to Ezra, over a period of about 845 years.

This means that the Adam and Eve story was last seen in writing by Helchiah or Azariah, therefore handed down verbally possibly by Azariah, and certainly by Seraiah and Ezra, and finally dictated by Ezra to five scribes. It is the five scribes' writings that we have today as Ezra's work. And the English is not even a literal translation . . . for instance, "without form and void" more literally would read "raging inundations and horrendous winds". . .

Now, through Ezra's reconstruction of Genesis, we are told many things:

1.   Because of the usage of "tree", "fruit", "serpent", "cherubim", and other words which were glyphs in the picture language of prehistory, it is evident that the Creation and Adam and Eve stories were probably originally written in the glyphs of Naga, the predominant Eastern Hemisphere language of 11,500 years ago. This language is nearly identical to ancient Mayan, and the progenitor of many languages, including Oriental and Polynesian tongues, Egyptian, Greek, and Yakut.

2.   Moses (and possibly Aaron) may have had access to these tablets, or Egyptian versions of them.

3.   Neither Moses nor Aaron knew how to read the ancient language, therefore read the glyphs quite literally.

4.   Not being able to read the symbolism of Naga glyphs, in addition to reading them literally, Moses and Aaron (and possibly Ezra) read into the Adam and Eve story the social and religious attitudes of their day. In that time woman was regarded as the root of all sin, a lowly creature, her birth recorded only as an exception, and basically being the cause of man's every downfall— a daily potential. This attitude persists in some religions even to our time.

Is it any wonder that Eve was shouldered with the responsibility for the downfall of all mankind, as a result of interpretations read into the Naga by Moses? And into Moses' reading by Ezra? Perhaps also it was read into the story by Egyptian priests long before Moses' time, and passed on to him as history.

5.   The fusing of two stories (P and J versions) into one to make the

story of Genesis I, II, and III may confuse "the man" with Adam. It is possible that Adam, being only nine generations ahead of Noah, with the time span of the Sudan Basin Polar Era covering 5,000 years, was not "the man" referred to in the creation, but his name and later experiences were merged with "the man's" story.

Remember, however, we are informed that Ezra dictated the entire history to five scribes from memory, and this work contains Genesis as we know it today. For him to recall from the archives of his mind what he did—as well as he did—certainly bespeaks of inspiration of a high order; but it also appears evident that he had no knowledge of the fact that 5,000 years transpired between Genesis I and Noah's flood. It is clear from 2 Ezdras 3:9 that Genesis I and Noah's flood represented two inundations, however, for while speaking of the two occasions, he says of Noah's flood: "And again in process of time thou broughtest the flood upon those that dwelt in the world, and destroyedst them."

Now, we mentioned before that the lineage of the high priests from Aaron to Ezra differs in number of generations (17 or 20) and names as presented in 1 and 2 Ezdras; and both differ in names from the book of Ezra. We also find differences in the lineages from Noah to Jesus (approximately 51 generations) in the Bible. Is it any wonder, therefore, that some generations could have been omitted in the Adam to Noah line? And the Aaron to Ezra line?

And in the light of the fact that, in addition to overwhelming scientific evidence, there are countless legends in the Asia-Pacific area, handed down from the inundation of 11,500 years ago, of a creation much like that of Genesis I and II, is it not possible that "the man" of the Genesis story became confused with Adam throughout the thousands of years, and through a succeeding tumble and inundation in Noah's time 6500 years ago? The miracle actually is that the whole story of "creation", and of Adam and Eve, is as undistorted as it is; being 11,500 years old, it has suffered through many debacles visited upon its guardians in the intervening years.

Because of the lack of resolving information, "the man" and Adam are kept as one in this translation- interpretation.

6.   The significant Naga glyphs given to us by Ezra through Moses' direct reading are:

Cherubims   Man   Fruit Rib   Woman   Serpent Adam's sleep Tree   Flaming Sword Our knowledge of Naga glyphs tells us that the tree (of life) symbolized a mother continent, a parent civilization lasting thousands of years longer than ours of today.

An unadorned serpent represented water, or the ocean; a serpent en-twined about the tree signified that the mother continent was sur-rounded by water. Genesis III, 15 actually describes Eve's heel on the serpent's head, showing her victory over the oceans.

Cherubims—which were not pretty, plump babies, but hybrid man and beast—were the glyphs for legs, or foundations, or underpin-nings. Instead of being placed in the garden of Eden, one was taken away; and a Naga or Maya reading of the Egyptian Book of the Dead shows that cherubims of the North, East, South, and West were taken away—meaning that the foundations of the mother continent, in all directions, were removed or destroyed.

The flaming sword was the symbol of fire and earthquake. The fire signified what all legends of these cataclysms call earth-fire, which is the molten layer below the earth's 60-mile thick shell breaking through to the surface during a tumble, a literal hell. It is most proba-bly the origin of man's concept of hell, as a matter of fact.

Now back to the tree: Fruit growing on that tree symbolized the orig-inal mankind which settled the mother continent ages before Adam and Eve. Their eating of the fruit tells us that they were descended from this original mankind of the continent. Eve eating first signifies that she was the generation after Adam, making her his daughter. His daughter!?

The glyph of the creation is even more revealing. There are three fig-ures represented in this picture; the top figure is the face of a sleeping or dead person (there were no separate symbols for death and sleep in Naga— both were represented as the same). The middle figure is shown as a male, and the bottom figure a female who is represented as the mother of all mankind. In addition, there are curved lines from the sleeping or dead person and the male middle figure to the bottom female figure.

This glyph has been interpreted to mean that the middle figure, a male, was put to sleep, shown by the top figure, and a rib (or ribs) removed from him (the ribs being the curved lines) and fashioned into the bottom figure, the female mother of all mankind. This fits beautifully with the story of Eve's creation, Adam therefore being both the male middle figure and the top figure, a sleeping (or dead) person.

There is a slight hitch to this story, however: the top figure, whether sleeping or dead, is depicted as a female! How could it be Adam, asleep, awake, dead, or alive? Moreover, in Naga the curved lines denote parentage rather than ribs; so, more reasonably, it appears that the top figure is a dead female, whose offspring by the male middle figure (Adam) was the bottom female figure (Eve), the mother of the Hebrews. So, in essence, the story as read from the glyphs would be that Adam and Eve, who lived in the Garden of Eden in the mother continent (tree), were descended from the original mankind (fruit) of that land, which incidentally was surrounded entirely by water (serpent around the tree). Eve was Adam's daughter, and he was a widower.

They realized that, in order to survive, they had to leave and never try to return, for the motherland was to be destroyed by a cataclysmic inundation. They left; and afterward, the continent (tree) was subjected to a fiery earthquake (flaming sword), during which it lost its foundations (cherubims), and sank beneath the ocean (serpent) which forever afterward walked over the sunken continent (on its belly).

So let's review the event—two cataclysms ago— and then apply our knowledge toward a representative translation-interpretation of Genesis I, II, and III. It may be the most accurate reading of a story written 11,500 years ago.

The Event - 11,500 Years Ago

Did you ever sit down for an evening at a card table with a 1000-piece puzzle? By yourself? It takes hours and hours to put it together, doesn't it, with trial, and error, and patience all playing their parts.

We're still trying out some of the as yet unfitted pieces in our world-wide puzzle, and we've been "at the table" since 1949. However, even though incomplete, it shows us a graphic representation of the earth's picture 11,500 years ago.

Look at a globe of the World. Pick out Longitude 90°W — Latitude 60 °N. This point is in the western part of the Hudson Bay.

Now hold the globe so that 90°W — 60°N is at the North Pole, on the axis of rotation. This was the configuration of the world between 18,500 years ago and 11,500 years ago. The North Polar ice cap formed the Laurentian Basin in Canada.

The continents, however, were not quite the same. There was a huge continent in the Atlantic Ocean area, which stretched from Iceland and England across the Atlantic to the Bahamas. The Gulf of Mexico and the Caribbean Sea did not exist — they were land at that time.

There was another continent in the Pacific — covering an area now ringed by the Hawaiian Islands, the Galapagos, Easter Island, Tahiti, the Solomons, and the Caroline Islands.

The Province of Ceylon held the major civilization of India. Egypt and the Holy Land were thriving mixtures of vegetation and civilization.

Greece — land of the Hellenes — was the home of a tall, blue-eyed, blonde race with standards of science and law unmatched to this day. The Amazon Basin was an inland sea — legends call it the Sea of Xarayes — and the mouth of the Amazon River was then a wide, seagoing connection between the Atlantic and Xarayes. The western coast of South America was not mountainous — the prehistoric city of Tiahuanaco, Peru, now at 12,500 feet above the Pacific, was then at sea level. It was a metropolis seaport, with a canal system for seagoing ships — as large as any we have today — traversing from the Pacific to the inland sea.

Astronomers of Tiahuanaco used telescopes like ours of today; and they had a huge satellite orbiting the earth -West to East, 449 times per year — which they used as a time standard, its orbit was so accurate. Ahoydia, now a suburb of Lucknow, was the capital of India. And the great navigators, the great scientists, the great explorers of the eastern hemisphere were the dark-eyed, dark-haired Mayans.

About 11,500 years ago — in 9,550 B.C., as dated by astronomers from Potsdam Observatory from writings in the ruins of Tiahuanaco — the 60-mile thick shell of the earth shifted its position once more in ¼ to ½ a day, 7,000 years after the previous shift. The North Pole moved southward, and the Sudan Basin in Africa shifted to the North Pole. This was the time which the Talmud states was the setting of the Pleiades below the horizon, when the Holy Land was moved into a "region of terrible cold" for many generations — actually for 5,000 years until Noah's flood, 6,500 years ago.

The equatorial pivot points were off the coast of mid-Chile and in mid-China, near the Yangtze, North of Viet Nam.

The great continent in the Pacific disappeared almost completely — what is now Easter Island, then on the edge of the continent, dropped to remain on the Pacific Ocean floor for 5,000 years — to be heaved up again in the cataclysm causing Noah's flood. What remained of the vast Pacific continent rolled to the South Pole, to be discovered by Mayan explorers as the last remains of their motherland — a "frozen reservoir of mud at the bottom of the earth," millions of square miles in area.

Of the great continent in the Atlantic, only a large island was left in the West, while the ocean between there and Gibraltar to the East was left shallow, muddy, and impassable to ships.

A thread of a clue concerning the great knowledge of that time came out when Captain Cook discovered the Polynesian Maori tribe in New Zealand in the 1700's. They told him of ancient legends of Saturn's rings — and they hadn't even heard of telescopes. Now you try to see those rings with your naked eyes — and you'll find out that it's impossible.

The evidence in Tiahuanaco shows that their great civilization was wiped out so suddenly that people were caught in the middle of their normal daytime activities by catastrophic inundation. Further, evidence shows that this fabulous city suffered the same fate as Easter Island: although the Rockies and Andes were started in this cataclysm, Tiahuanaco was buried under the Pacific, to remain there for 5,000 years, then to be heaved up to its present altitude of 12,500 feet in the last cataclysm 6,500 years ago. So the cataclysm of 11,500 years ago saw the Hudson Bay and the opposite polar area just southwest of Australia both roll to the equator on opposite sides of the Earth, and the Sudan Basin region roll to the North Pole, to remain there for the next 5000 years. While this shift was occurring, taking only ¼ to ½ a day to complete itself, the earth's oceans and atmosphere, through angular momentum, kept rotating in their normal direction during most of the shift, with the oceans violently inundating most of the lands of the Earth, and the atmosphere bringing unimaginable hurricanes of up to supersonic wind velocities. Whole continents were subjected to tremendous upheavals and earthquakes. The molten layer below the earth's 60-mile thick shell broke through the shell in places all over the world, and was thereafter called "earth-fire" by the pitiful few who survived. . . . .

The oceans and winds took six days after the start of the cataclysm to resolve their holocaustic wars on the surface of the earth, and on the seventh day began to settle down to 5,000 years of normal complacency. The two-mile thick ice caps of the Laurentian Basin and the Indian Ocean, having shifted from their polar homes and started a new course of revolving equatorially, proceeded to melt at tremendous speeds in the torrid heat, carving great grooves in the mountains as the rushing, gushing, swirling water and ice overwhelmed everything in their paths. The great amounts of moisture being poured into the atmosphere were to shroud the Torrid Zone in a dark fog for many years during several generations. The oceans rose some 200 feet all over the world with the sudden melting of the ice caps, as they do after each cataclysm.

The end of the Laurentian Ice Age, and the start of the "Old Stone Age" was complete.

The Mayan tongue lived on in scattered remnants: Polynesian tongues, Greek, Yakut, Egyptian, Eskimo tongues, Nomadic, Oriental, German, American Indian - just about all languages. The resurrection from the waters — Tau — lived on in many stories of a man who survived, later to become Ta'aroa, Tongaroa, Taroa'a, depending on which tribe's legend you find.

Adam and Eve could have sprung from the same story. Who knows?

GENESIS: 4,500,000,000 YEARS AGO

THIS REGENESIS: 11,500 YEARS AGO

Both in the Bible

A translation-interpretation of Genesis I, II, and III, from a reconstruction of what the Naga must have been to give us the chapters as we have had them in English; then retranslating directly from Naga to English, bypassing Greek and Hebrew.

The Book of Genesis - 1,2,3

C hapters I, II, and III

I.

1.   ¶ In the beginning (4.5 billion years ago) the universe was created in God's great design. Included was our Sun, and our planet Earth.

2.   And during one of the many cataclysms that occurred during the earth's history (this one being 11,500 years ago), the earth's lands were all inundated with raging waters, and ravaged by horrendous winds; and the oceans were all dark with muddiness. And the ill wind thundered over the troubled waters also.

3.   And as the storms abated, sunlight came back to the face of the earth, as God intended.

4.   And, while the holocaust was abating, once more darkness and sunlight were reestablished and distinguishable, and it was good.

5.   And sunlight was again daytime, and darkness again nighttime, in accordance with God's design; and evening and morning made one day.

6.   ¶ Again, God's original design was that there be a sky between the clouds and oceans;

7.   And in accordance with God's design, the heavens were reestablished, in that the sky again stood between the clouds and the oceans, as the onslaught of the great storms abated.

8.   And God's heavens were indeed reestablished; and that evening and morning were the beginning of the second day.

9.   ¶ And God's design was that the lands would not be entirely covered by the oceans as they were immediately following a cataclysm, so the disrupted oceans, now settling, drained off the higher lands.

10.   And, in accordance with God's design, the dry land was earth, and the waters oceans, and once again it was reestablished and good, as God intended.

11.   And since God's design was that the earth should bring forth grass and herbs, yielding their seed, and the fruit yielding fruit containing its seed; and the earth was again reestablished.

12.   Therefore the earth, being reestablished, brought forth grass and herbs, yielding their seed, and the fruit tree yielding fruit containing its seed; and it was good, as God intended.

13.   And the evening and the morning were the start of the third day.

14.   ¶ In accordance with God's design, there were normally lights in the heavens, which served to indicate months, and seasons, and days, and years;

15.   Also they served to furnish light on the earth, as God intended.

16.   And as the great fog lifted, and the clouds broke, the Sun and Moon reappeared, and also the stars;

17.   And once again, as God intended, they shone from the heavens;

18.   And the Sun and Moon again were able to divide light and darkness, which was good.

19.   And the evening and the morning were the start of the fourth day.

20.   And it was God's will that some of every creature living, and bird flying, should survive the cataclysmic inundation.

21.   Surviving then were great whales, and every living creature of the sea, and every kind of winged fowl; and it was as God intended,

and good.

22. And they were blessed with God's original design to be fruitful, and reproduce, and replenish the oceans with sea life and the air with fowl.

23. And the evening and the morning were the start of the fifth day.

24. ¶ And it was God's will that some of every creature, cattle, and creeping thing, and beast of the earth, should survive the cataclysmic inundation;

25. Surviving then were the beasts, the cattle, and every thing that creeps on the earth; and it was as God intended, and good.

26. And in accordance with God's design, man, who was created in the image God intended, also was to survive, and have dominion over the fowl of the air, and over the cattle, and over all the earth, and over every creeping thing that creeps on the earth.

27. So it was God's design that man, who was created in the image God intended, both male and female, would survive the cataclysmic inundation.

28. And they were blessed with God's original design to be fruitful, and multiply, and replenish the earth, and control it; and have dominion over the fish of the sea, and over the fowl of the air, and over every living thing that moves upon the earth.

29. ¶ And God's design was that man, being given every herb bearing seed, which is upon the face of all the earth, and every tree, in which is the fruit of a tree yielding seed; to man it should be for food.

30. And to every beast of the earth, and to every fowl of the air, and to every thing that creeps on the earth, wherein there is life, God's design was that green herbs shall serve for food; and it was as God intended.

31. And every thing which survived, was as God had originally created, and still was in God's design, and was good. And the evening and the morning were the beginning of the sixth day.

II.

1.   ¶ Thus the heavens and the earth were reestablished, all the host of them.

2.   And on the seventh day the recovery from the holocaust and flood were complete; and the seventh day brought rest from the fight for survival against the holocaust and its aftereffects.

3.   And the seventh day brought God's blessed peace, as the holocaust had abated, leaving those of his creation who survived.

4.   ¶ These are the same regenerations of the heavens and of the earth as they were reestablished after the tumble previous to the one of this story, when the Lord God reestablished the earth and the heavens.

5.   And every plant of the field before that cataclysm was in the earth, and every herb of the field before it grew. For the Lord God had not brought rain upon the earth in this region, and there was not a man to till the ground.

6.   But there was this cataclysm, and great inundations arose over the earth.

7.   And it was God's will that man should rise up from the earth, and keep the breath of life, and remain a living soul. This is his story.

8.   ¶ And it was God's will, after a cataclysm, that a continent eastward be established, and there in Eden lived the man of this story.

9.   And from this land grew other civilizations, on other lands, with the motherland in the midst of all being the seat of wisdom, of all knowledge, both good and evil.

10.   And the inundation destroyed Eden, and left only its four offspring lands.

(Note: The next four verses are probably incorrect, with the true description locked in correct translations of Egypt's "Book of the Dead", and the missing portion of the Piri Reis map.)

11.   The first land is near the river Pison, which includes the whole land of Havilah, where there is gold;

12.   And the gold of that land is good: there is bdellium and the onyx

stone.

13. And the second land is near the river Gihon: the same land which includes the whole land of Ethiopia.

14. And the third land is near the river Hiddekel: that is the land toward the east of Assyria. And the fourth land is near the river Euphrates.

15. And it was in God's province that the man was of Eden, where he lived and toiled.

16. And he was descended from the original mankind which settled that motherland.

17. And God's design was that the man was warned: although the motherland was the source of all knowledge, both good and evil, if he stay therein, surely he would die.

18. ¶ And it was God's design that the man should not be alone, therefore a mate should be his;

19. And since God had originally created every beast of the field, and fowl of the air, and in his time Adam had named each one;

20. And Adam gave names to all cattle, and to the fowl of the air, and to every beast of the field; but for Adam there was no mate.

21. For Adam's mate had died, after giving birth to a child of Adam;

22. And the child of the man was a female, made in the image God intended;

23. And Adam said, this child is bone of my bone, and flesh of my flesh; and she grew into womanhood.

24. Therefore, the man was both father and mother to her, and she abode with him, as they were one flesh.

25. And the climate there was warm, requiring little or no clothing.

III.

1. ¶ Now at the time of the beginning of this story, the oceans were in their normal state of quietness; and it was known to the woman of this story that she was not descended from any of the peoples of the

lands which sprang from the mother continent;

2. And God's design was that the woman would learn that the people of the offspring lands would live on,

3. But the people of the motherland, from whom she had descended, would surely all die.

4. And she knew that in spite of the impending inundation, she would not surely die;

5. For God's design was that from the day she was born, she was descended from the original mankind of the motherland, and was destined to know all, to discern both good and evil.

6. And the woman, being of the motherland, and being wise and good, knew that both she and her father were

descended from the original mankind of the motherland.

7. And they both were wise, and had lived the good life; and it was that time of the year when some clothing was needed for warmth.

8. And in the cool of those days, when they were wondering to which of the offspring lands they should go, and God's presence was felt strongly by them,

9. Adam felt God's call,

10. And said, I have heard God's warning since the summer, and have feared, for I knew not where to find refuge;

11. And God's warning had come to him in the summer, as a warning to leave the land of his ancestors.

12. And the man said, the woman who is my daughter, and descended of my ancestors, gave me this knowledge;

13. And asked her, What gift of knowledge has God given you? And the woman said, I am of your ancestors and inherit their wisdom; and the coming inundations of the oceans has been made known to me;

14. And God's design was that the oceans would so inundate the lands, and drown all cattle, and all beasts of the field, and bury all dust,

15. And God has thus given me victory over the oceans, such that the seed of future generations is in you and me, for the oceans will drown all others.

16.   And God's design was that although the inundation would greatly multiply her sorrows, she would even so bring forth children, as her love would be for her husband, and his for her.

17.   And unto Adam it was God's will that he heed the words of his daughter, and God's warning that though they be descendants of original mankind of the motherland, they should leave it, as it was destined for destruction, and were they to stay, surely they would regret it;

18.   And where Adam was to go, the land would be difficult to farm, with thorns and thistles abounding; and even so the herb of the field was to be their food.

19.   By his own toil and sweat he was destined to fight the fight for survival after the inundation, even to the end of his days, when he would return to mother Earth, as it was Earth man came from, and unto Earth he shall return.

20.   And after the inundation, Adam therefore made the woman his wife, and called her Eve, as she was to be the mother of all living from the motherland.

21.   And, again after the inundation, as they were in a colder climate, it was God's design as part of their survival that they make coats of skins, and be clothed.

22.   ¶ And it was God's design that Adam should take with him the knowledge of good and evil from the motherland as he put forth and left in order to live;

23.   Therefore, in accordance with God's will, he left the garden of Eden, to survive and live from the soil where he was to go.

24.   So the man left; and the garden of Eden was subjected to a cataclysm of earthquake and fire, and the motherland lost its foundations, and sank beneath the oceans.

Conclusion

India...

Greece...

Egypt...

When Indra, King of the Gods, had destroyed the Titan who held the waters of the earth captive in his entrails, he returned to the heights of the Central Mountain with the song of the rains and running waters in his ears. But where his dwelling once stood, he saw only ruins and ashes. So he summoned Visvakarman, god of works and arts, and asked him to build another palace to match his powers. The architect set to work; soon towers, buildings, and gardens rose among lakes and woods. Indra urged him forward impatiently. Each day he called for some fresh marvel, new delight for the eyes, walls more imperial, pavilions more richly adorned, statues greater in number and cunning. A fever seemed to burn in him. And Visvakarman, exhausted by his labors, decided to lay a complaint before the Creator of the world. Brahma received him, gave ear, approved, and went to plead his cause before Vishnu, the supreme Being. Help was promised.

Soon a young Brahman appeared at the King's palace and demanded audience. Charmed by the light of his eyes, Indra granted his request. "Oh King," said the messenger, "thy palace shall be the noblest of all." These words were sweet to Indra's ears, and he rejoiced. Vishnu's messenger continued: "It shall be the noblest of the palaces which the Indras before thyself sought to build." The King became uneasy. "Dost thou say that there were other Indras, other Visvakarmans before ourselves, other palaces before mine?"

"Indeed yes," the youth answered. "I have seen them."

"Moreover I have seen the world arise and vanish, arise and vanish again, like a tortoise's shell coming out of Infinite ocean and sinking back. I was present at the dawn and the twilight of the Cycles, past counting in their numbers, nor could I count all the Indras and Visvakarmans, even the Vishnus and Brahmas, following one another without end."

Brahmavaivarta Purana and Krishnajanma Khanda "O Solon, Solon, you Hellenes are but children. . . .

There is no old doctrine handed down among you by ancient tradition nor any science which is hoary with age, and I will tell you the reason behind this. There have been and will be again many destructions of mankind arising out of many causes, the greatest having been brought about by earth-fire and inundation.

Whatever happened either in your country or ours or in any other country of which we are informed, any action which is noble and great or in any other way remarkable which has taken place, all that has been inscribed long ago in our temple records, whereas you and other nations did not keep imperishable records. And then, after a period of time, the usual inundation visits like a pestilence and leaves only those of you who are destitute of letters and education. And thus you have to begin over again as children and know nothing of what happened in ancient times either among us or among yourselves."

"As for those genealogies of yours which you have related to us, they are no better than tales of children; for in the first place, you remember one deluge only, whereas there were a number of them. And in the next place there dwelt in your land, which you do not know, the fairest and noblest race of men that ever lived of which you are but a seed or remnant. And this was not known to you because for many generations the survivors of that destruction made no records."

Plato: Timaeus

(Spoken by a priest of Egypt)

Therefore will not we fear, though the earth be removed, and though the mountains be carried into the midst of the sea;

Though the waters thereof roar and be troubled, though the mountains shake with the swelling thereof.

Psalm 46

The Author

Mr. Thomas attended Dartmouth College and Columbia University, receiving his degree in Electrical Engineering from the latter in 1943.

As a result of his research since 1949, Mr. Thomas has become recognized as the world's leading authority in the field of cataclysmic geology and its relationship to uniformitarian geology.

In 1959 he applied his findings to the possibility of earthquake prediction, and at a seminar in November, 1959 issued the results of his studies. He then accurately forecast the months, years, and locations of the major African and Chilean earthquakes of 1960, the Iranian earthquake of 1962, the Jugoslavian earthquake of 1963, and further predicted that California would have no major earthquakes for the following five years.

His correlation research in the fields of stratigraphy, vertebrate palaeontology, radiology, oceanography, glacio-ogly, seismology, palaeophilology, earth magnetism, anthropology, and other related fields, has demonstrated that the cataclysmic geology theories as presented by DeLuc in 1779 and Cuvier in 1812 are definitely more acceptable than they have been previously within international scientific circles.

Mr. Thomas' definitive efforts in integrating the various earth sciences have distinguished him as the only American today with such a specialized scientific forte.

His research in palaeosciences has led to new explanations of such enigmas as the Pyramid of Khufu at Gizeh, the ancient cities of Tiahuanaco and Baalbek, and the giant statues of Easter Island.

A little bit of knowledge
Can be a dangerous thing;
Or it can be a vibrant seed
Giving rise to verdant forests
And awakening sleeping giants.

Ancient Myths – The Echo of Forgotten Worlds

There is a strange comfort in treating ancient myths as nothing more than stories, symbolic parables meant to guide the living. That comfort begins to dissolve when you line those myths up side by side, when you hear them told in the voices of people who could never have met, separated by oceans and millennia, yet repeating the same warnings in different words. They speak of water swallowing the land, of fire falling from the sky, of darkness lasting longer than night should, and of a sky that suddenly tilts. These are not the slow, patient changes we have come to associate with geology and climate. They are violent, sudden, and personal. They are the memory of survivors, accounts dressed in the robes of gods and monsters, warnings carried across generations by story when there was no science left to explain them.

In the river valleys of Mesopotamia, the Sumerians wrote of Utnapishtim, chosen by the gods to survive a coming flood. He built a great vessel, carrying his family, animals, and the seeds of the old world to safety. His story mirrors the later Hebrew tale of Noah almost detail for detail, forty days of rain, a dove sent out to search for land, a mountaintop where the ark finally rests. In India, the story takes the form of Manu, warned by a great fish, the god Vishnu himself, of an oncoming deluge. In Greece, it is Deucalion and Pyrrha, surviving Zeus's destruction of humankind by flood and repopulating the Earth with stones thrown over their shoulders. Among the Hopi, far from any ocean, the Fourth World ended in water, and the few who survived did so in hollow reeds. In each of these accounts, there is a warning, an escape, destruction, and renewal. Whether the vessel was an ark of wood, a great fish, or a hollow reed, the pattern is unmistakable.

Yet water was only one of the elements in these cycles of destruction. Fire, too, played its part in ending worlds. The Hopi tell of the Blue Star Kachina, a celestial sign that will appear before the sky shakes, the Earth trembles, and fire sweeps across the land. In the Norse vision of Ragnarök, the fire giant Surtr sets the world ablaze before the Sun goes black and the stars vanish. The Aztecs spoke of previous "Suns," entire worlds destroyed and remade, one of which perished when flaming serpents rained from the heavens. Across the Pacific, the Maori remembered a time of "fires that ran," when meteors or comets blazed through the sky, scorching the Earth and boiling the seas.

The end by fire often gave way to an aftermath of cold and darkness. Egyptian records like the Ipuwer Papyrus speak of a world thrown into chaos, famine spreading, and the Sun failing to shine. The Aztecs remembered the "Sun of Darkness," when the world was swallowed by night. Among the Norse, Fimbulwinter, three years without summer, was the prelude to the final destruction, a description eerily close to the "impact winter" modern science associates with massive asteroid strikes. Even the Inuit tell of a time when the Sun rose in a different place, the air turned heavy, and the cold deepened until survival became impossible.

Sometimes these changes were described as a tilting of the sky itself. Polynesian traditions recall that the heavens once pressed low upon the Earth until the hero Māui pushed them upward, but other tellings remember the sky tilting suddenly, altering the stars' positions. African peoples like the Dogon and the San recount a day when the Sun moved and the balance of the world shifted. In China's myth of Nüwa, the sky cracks and leans, unleashing floods and fire upon the land. Even the Bible carries the echo in the Book of Isaiah, describing an Earth that "reels to and fro like a drunkard" and will "fall, and not rise again."

Through all of these stories, symbols recur like a hidden code. Serpents and dragons, often fiery or winged, may be memories of comets or strange electrical phenomena in the sky. Boats and arks stand for survival and preservation, whether literal or symbolic. Trees of life appear only to be burned or destroyed, marking the end of an age. Mountains serve as refuges or the first points of safety after the waters recede. These symbols persist because they speak across language and time; they are memory devices meant to survive even when the science of the events is lost.

If one were to map these myths across the globe, the points would cluster in ways that defy chance. They appear in floodplains, yes, but also high on mountain plateaus, in dry inland deserts, and on remote volcanic islands. If you then overlay known geological evidence, impact craters, sudden sea-level changes, and layers of debris from ancient floods, the overlap is too great to ignore. The Epic of Gilgamesh aligns with the flooding of the Persian Gulf basin at the end of the Younger Dryas. The Hopi's transition from the Fourth World could fit within the window of a Holocene impact event. Polynesian accounts of a sky tilt parallel the recalculations ancient astronomers would have had to make after a rapid shift in the Earth's rotation.

Modern thinking has trained us to separate myth from science, as though they occupy different realities. But for ancient peoples, they were one and the same. Myths were not bedtime stories; they were operating manuals for survival. A Greek hearing the story of Deucalion did not need to know the mechanics of orbital debris to understand that when the signs appeared, the sky trembling, the Sun changing its path, the waters withdrawing, it was time to seek higher ground. The Maya did not record the motions of Venus for poetry alone; they did so because the sky was their calendar, their clock, and their warning system.

Today we congratulate ourselves on our science while ignoring the very warnings it confirms. In ice cores, crater fields, and the magnetic memory of rocks, we see the same patterns the myths describe. In the stones of ancient monuments, we find alignments and markings that suggest the ancients were not primitive at all, but survivors of something they knew would happen again. The stories they left us are not superstitions, they are data, encoded in a form meant to outlast empires. And the message that comes through, even after thousands of years of retelling, is simple: it happened before. It will happen again.

FLOOD MYTHS BY CULTURE

Mesopotamia & Near East

- Ziusudra (Sumerian) / Eridu Genesis
- Atrahasis (Akkadian)
- Utnapishtim – *Epic of Gilgamesh* (Babylonian)
- Xisuthros (Berosus' Hellenized account)
- Noah / Nuh (Abrahamic traditions)
- Yima's Vara (Avestan/Persian, cataclysm survival)

Mediterranean & Europe

- Deucalion & Pyrrha (Greek)
- Ogyges' Flood (Greek)
- Cantre'r Gwaelod – Sunken Kingdom (Welsh)
- Ys / Ker-Ys – Sunken City (Breton)
- Lyonesse – Drowned Land (Cornish)
- Bergelmir & the Flood of Ymir's Blood (Norse)
- Ragnarök Deluge (Norse)

- Flood traditions in Irish *Lebor Gabála Érenn*

South Asia

- Manu & Matsya (Vedic/Hindu)
- Satyavrata Manu (Puranic variants)
- Kumari Kandam Sea Inundations (Tamil legend)
- Jātaka Flood Tales (Buddhist)

East & Southeast Asia

- Great Flood of Gun–Yu (China)
- Nüwa Mends the Sky (China)
- Fuxi & Nüwa as Flood Survivors (China)
- Miao/Hmong Great Flood
- Ainu Great Flood (Japan)
- Sơn Tinh vs. Thủy Tinh – Annual Floods (Vietnam)
- Lumawig and the Deluge (Ifugao/Igorot, Philippines)
- Kaptan & Maguayan Deluge (Visayan, Philippines)
- Dayak Flood Traditions (Borneo, Indonesia)

Oceania & Australia

- Nu◇u (Hawaiian)
- Ruatapu & the Great Wave (Māori)
- Djanggawul Flood (Yolŋu, Australia)
- Tiddalik the Frog – Release of Waters (SE Australia)
- Wandjina Bring the Flood (Worrorra/Ngarinyin)

Africa

- Olókun's Flood (Yoruba, West Africa)
- Faro Saves the World from Flood (Mande, Mali)

- Kwaya/Ikoma/Masai Flood Traditions (East Africa)
- Khoikhoi Great Flood (Southern Africa)

Indigenous North America

- Haida & Tlingit Flood (NW Coast)
- Coast Salish Flood (Salish Sea)
- Nuu-chah-nulth Flood (Vancouver Island)
- Kwakwaka'wakw & Tsimshian Floods (NW Coast)
- Hopi: Second World Destroyed by Flood (Southwest)
- Navajo Deluge in Emergence Cycle (Southwest)
- Pima/O'odham Flood – Montezuma Survives (Southwest)
- Mandan Flood (Plains)
- Ojibwe/Nanabozho Flood (Great Lakes)
- Menominee Flood (Great Lakes)
- Mi'kmaq Flood (Atlantic)
- Lenape/Delaware Flood (Atlantic)
- Choctaw & Caddo Floods (Southeast)
- Creek/Muscogee Flood (Southeast)
- Inuit/Alaska Flood Traditions (Arctic)

Central & South America

- *Popol Vuh*: Destruction of the 'Wooden People' by Flood (Maya)
- Coxcox & Xochiquetzal (Aztec)
- Mixtec Flood (Apoala)
- Zapotec Flood Legends
- Tarascan/Purépecha Flood
- Unu Pachakuti (Inca)
- Chibchacum's Flood & Bochica Drains the Waters (Muisca)
- Cañari Brothers Saved on a Mountain (Ecuador)
- Tupí-Guaraní Flood – Monan Sends the Deluge (Amazon)

- Trentren Vilu vs. Caicai Vilu – Deluge (Mapuche)

Part 2: What We Know Now

Introduction to Part 2

When the CIA finally "released" The Adam and Eve Story decades after they had locked it away, what they gave the public was not the book Chan Thomas published in 1963. It was a stripped-down, 57-page fragment, a surgical removal of whatever they deemed too sensitive. Missing were entire chapters, appendices, and survival sections. Missing were detailed descriptions of the next catastrophe as Thomas envisioned it. Missing, too, were his connections between the geological record, the ancient myths, and the physical preparations he believed were already underway in certain corners of the world.

If this was simply fringing pseudoscience, there would have been no need for redaction. Governments don't waste resources censoring nonsense. They might mock it, discredit it, or ignore it entirely, but they don't hide it for three decades and then release only a sterilized sliver. That's not the behavior of an intelligence agency treating a harmless theory. That's the behavior of an agency managing information that has strategic implications.

In the public version, the bones of the theory remain. Thomas still describes a world where the crust can slip over the mantle in a matter of hours or days, pulling the continents into new latitudes. He still paints the picture of roaring winds, mile-high tsunamis, and erased continents. But the details, the connective tissue that ties this vision to specific dates, events, or evidence, are gone. What remains is enough to spark curiosity, but not enough to galvanize the public into serious preparation. It is the equivalent of showing you the cover of a survival manual and tearing out the pages with the actual instructions.

These matters because the missing content is where the threat becomes real. The stripped-down version is easy to treat as a curiosity, a relic from the Cold War era when the U.S. government was obsessed with doomsday scenarios. But the moment you remember that Hapgood, Einstein, and others had already been debating sudden crust displacement; that ancient myths from every continent describe nearly identical cataclysms; and that modern geological evidence has since vindicated many of these claims , the classification starts to look less like caution and more like control.

When information is hidden, it's rarely because it's false. It's because the people holding it believe it's true enough to matter, and dangerous enough to keep quiet. In the context of the 1960s, this was not an idle intellectual exercise. The United States government was actively studying continuity-of-government plans, how to keep leadership alive in the event of nuclear war, cosmic impact, or planetary catastrophe. They were boring deep underground facilities, mapping safe zones, and tracking the same astronomical cycles that ancient builders encoded into stone.

It's worth remembering that the CIA did not simply classify Thomas's work, they also kept it classified through an era when cataclysm research exploded in private circles. Hapgood's later work had been softened, with timelines stretched and the urgency diluted. The public narrative shifted toward slow change. And in the meantime, the technological capacity to confirm or disprove the most radical version of these theories, satellite mapping, deep ice cores, precision carbon dating, quietly grew in the hands of governments and select institutions. By the time the CIA released the sanitized text, much of the original urgency had been defused. Thomas himself was gone. The intellectual climate had shifted. And yet, when you read between the lines, the implications remain. The mechanics he describes are not science fiction. They are rooted in plausible geophysics, in the interaction between the crust, the mantle, and the shifting balance of polar ice and rotational forces. The idea that the crust can move suddenly is no longer dismissed outright; it's discussed quietly in certain geoscience circles under different names, with different framing. The words "catastrophic crust displacement" may be avoided, but the research into rapid pole movement, geomagnetic excursions, and abrupt climate shifts continues.

This is why it matters now. Fifty years later, we have far more evidence than Thomas ever did. The ice cores from Greenland and Antarctica show abrupt temperature swings of 10–15 degrees Celsius in less than a decade, sometimes in a handful of years. Magnetic field measurements confirm that the poles can shift hundreds of kilometers in a human lifetime, and that the field is weakening faster than predicted. Geological surveys show sudden sea-level changes, massive tsunami deposits far inland, and megafaunal extinctions that happened within the memory span of our species.

The missing pages of The Adam and Eve Story almost certainly contained Thomas's attempt to connect these dots, to tie ancient warnings to the geological record and present them as an immediate concern. That kind of synthesis is exactly what intelligence agencies prize and fear, the act of taking disparate, publicly available data points and assembling them into a coherent, actionable picture. A single academic paper on pole movement is not a threat. A single archaeological site showing sudden abandonment is not a threat. But the combination, the pattern, can shift public perception, alter priorities, and even threaten stability.

By truncating the book, the CIA didn't erase the theory. They neutered it. They left just enough for curious readers to chase, knowing that without the full map, most would get lost in speculation. But they also ensured that the version people read in the future would lack the specifics that might have driven urgent preparation or independent verification. The classified sections could be quietly absorbed into their own planning, folded into scenario work that the public would never see.

We live now in a time when the kind of evidence Thomas hinted at is pouring in from multiple, independent directions, and that is exactly what makes the truncation worth remembering. If Thomas's original work was dangerous enough to lock away in 1966, what does it mean that science has since confirmed many of the background facts? What does it mean that we can now track, in real time, the kinds of changes he described, not over geological epochs, but within our own lifetimes?

The answer is simple, and uncomfortable: the redactions in The Adam and Eve Story are not ancient history. They are an open wound in our collective knowledge. They remind us that certain truths are still considered too disruptive to release without control. They are proof that information about the cycles of destruction and renewal on this planet has never been evenly shared, and likely never will be.

If you want to understand why this book still matters, look not at what remains, but at what was taken away. And then look at the modern evidence , the floods, the fires, the magnetic shifts, the buried cities, the cosmic debris fields , and ask yourself how much longer this pattern can hold before the next sudden turn of the Earth's skin sweeps the old world away.

In the decades since Thomas wrote The Adam and Eve Story, the landscape of discovery has shifted in ways he could never have imagined , but in directions that would have confirmed his instincts. Independent researchers, working far from the gatekeepers of official science, have been quietly piecing together the same picture from different starting points. The puzzle is scattered across disciplines, geology, archaeology, astronomy, climate science, and yet the shapes of the pieces match.

From the geologists came the revelations of abrupt transitions in the ice ccores,sharp, vertical jumps in temperature and precipitation that could not be explained by slow, incremental climate change. In the Greenland cores, you can see the Younger Dryas boundary like a scar, a sudden crash into cold, then a rapid surge back to warmth. These are not the gentle slopes of the climate graphs they show in classrooms; these are cliffs.

The archaeologists, in turn, began unearthing sites that didn't fit the textbook timeline of civilization. Gobekli Tepe in Turkey, deliberately buried, perfectly preserved, and aligned to the movements of the heavens, emerged as the smoking gun of a lost world. Its construction dates back over 11,000 years, to the very end of the Younger Dryas, as if the survivors of some great trauma were leaving behind a coded message for whoever came next.

Astronomers, too, have found their way into the story, not through mysticism but through hard observation. The Comet Research Group's work on the Younger Dryas Impact Hypothesis ties a cosmic collision to that same period of chaos. Nanodiamonds, microspherules, meltglass , all the fingerprints of something violent from above , have been found in strata all over the world, matching perfectly with the timing of the great melt and the flooding of coastlines. Meanwhile, the climate scientists , at least the ones not shackled to political agendas , have been mapping patterns that extend far beyond the industrial age. They can see now that Earth's magnetic field has weakened before, rapidly, and that such times often coincide with massive environmental upheaval. Some, like Ben Davidson, have drawn direct connections between these geomagnetic excursions, solar outbursts, and the kind of sudden planetary changes Thomas described.

The result is a convergence, separate lines of evidence, separate research, separate methods, all pointing to the same conclusion: the Earth is not a stable platform. It is a machine with gears that slip, springs that release, cycles that run on a clock far older and less forgiving than any human institution. Thomas glimpsed that machine. Others, in the years since, have measured their parts in more detail.

Together, they have built a case that the missing pages of The Adam and Eve Story would have fit into perfectly, perhaps too perfectly for the comfort of those who prefer an unprepared public.

Randall Carlson – The Keeper of the Patterns

Randall Carlson has been called many things, a rogue scholar, a heretic in the house of geology, a teacher of forbidden history, but at his core he is a master of patterns. He doesn't treat the landscape as a static backdrop. He treats it as a crime scene, frozen mid-disaster, waiting for someone with the right eye to reconstruct what happened. And when you follow him into the scablands of eastern Washington or stand with him on the rim of a coulee that stretches for miles, you start to see what he sees: this was not carved by wind, rain, and the slow crawl of time. This was sudden. This was violent.

Carlson's specialty is the megaflood, the kind of event so far outside modern human experience that we have trouble accepting it even when standing in the middle of its aftermath. Across North America, there are scars so large they can only be truly appreciated from the air: vast ripple marks taller than houses, canyons with no modern rivers to explain them, and isolated boulders the size of small buildings stranded far from any logical source.

The orthodox explanation for much of this , the Missoula Floods , already admits to catastrophic water releases at the end of the last ice age, as glacial lakes burst and sent torrents roaring across the continent. But Carlson has spent decades showing that these were not isolated, single events. They were part of a series, a barrage, a pulse of destruction tied to the rapid melting and destabilization of the ice sheets. In some cases, the water moved at speeds and volumes beyond anything modern hydrology has modeled, hundreds of feet deep, hundreds of miles wide, traveling at freeway speeds, stripping soil down to bedrock.

The channeled scablands of Washington State are the most famous example, a bizarre labyrinth of dry channels, coulees, and giant pot-holes stretching for hundreds of miles. Mainstream geology long resisted the idea that they were carved in days or weeks, but the evidence has piled up too high to ignore. Carlson traces these features with maps, drone footage, and boots-on-the-ground surveying, showing how water once poured across this landscape in impossible quantities, leaving behind streamlined hills known as drumlins, immense gravel bars, and gravel "dunes" that make no sense without floods on a scale no modern river could produce.

What makes Carlson's work relevant to The Adam and Eve Story is not just that he proves cataclysms happen , it's that he demonstrates they happen within the timescale of human memory. The Missoula Floods ended only about 12,000 years ago, squarely within the Younger Dryas event that the Comet Research Group has tied to an extraterrestrial impact. In other words, the same period when global temperatures plunged and then spiked, ice sheets collapsed, and coast-lines were redrawn , the same window of time that Thomas and Hap-good both placed their last "crust shift" or pole movement.

Carlson's megaflood evidence also destroys the comforting notion of gradualism , the idea that landscapes are shaped only by slow erosion and gentle change. A single flood can do the work of hundreds of thousands of years of "normal" geological processes. And when you start seeing these features not just in the Northwest, but across the Midwest, in the Hudson Valley, even in parts of Alaska and Canada, the scale of the destruction becomes global in implication.

This is the keeper-of-the-patterns role Carlson plays: he connects the dots between distant places and events, revealing that the scars of cat-aclysm are not isolated anomalies but repeating signatures. To him, the drumlins of New York and the coulees of Washington are chap-ters of the same story , a story of sudden, repeated upheaval that can erase civilizations and leave only the bones of their cities buried under layers of silt and gravel.

Carlson doesn't claim to know the exact trigger of these events, but he keeps the possibilities open: massive glacial outburst floods alone, or floods triggered by rapid pole movement, or the cascading effects of an impact event breaking the ice dams. What matters, in his telling, is that the planet can and does shift gears abruptly. When it does, the forces unleashed are beyond anything our infrastructure, agriculture, or political systems are built to handle.

In the light of Thomas's book, Carlson's work becomes a living demonstration of what the CIA-redacted sections might have contained: tangible, undeniable evidence that our planet's surface has been violently rearranged in the recent past, and that such events are not the realm of myth but of hard, measurable fact. The scablands are not a legend. They're not an allegory. They're a warning carved into the bedrock of a continent, one that can only be ignored by those who refuse to see the patterns staring at them in the face.

Carlson's work doesn't stop at reading the scars in stone and soil. He reads the sky as well, because to him the two are part of the same record. The Earth is not an isolated stage, it's part of a cosmic theater, and the actors are the planets, the Sun, and whatever debris the Solar System sweeps through on its endless journey around the galactic center. He studies these cycles the way a seasoned hunter studies the seasons: not as abstract numbers, but as patterns that predict when the next change will come.

In Carlson's lectures, he lays out timelines measured in thousands and tens of thousands of years, showing how planetary alignments, orbital variations, and precessional cycles have coincided with periods of environmental chaos. This is not astrology dressed up in scientific jargon, it's astronomy applied to survival. When the tilt of the Earth, the wobble of its axis, and the position of the planets align in certain ways, the stress on our planet's systems can spike. Combine those stresses with an already weakened magnetic field, and the conditions for catastrophe begin to stack.

This is where ancient sky-watching enters the picture. Carlson argues, and backs with detailed architectural and mathematical analysis, that many megalithic sites were designed not just as temples or calendars, but as instruments for tracking these long cycles. He points to alignments in structures from Stonehenge to the Great Pyramids to the serpent mounds of North America, all marking solstices, equinoxes, lunar standstills, and key precessional points. These were not superstitions. They were data points, benchmarks that allowed ancient cultures to predict the return of destructive events.

Sacred geometry, in this framework, is not mystical decoration. It is a language of proportion and number that encodes astronomical knowledge into stone. Ratios found in these structures, the golden ratio, the square root of two, pi , are not arbitrary. They appear in orbital mechanics, in the relationship between Earth and Moon, and in the scaling of celestial cycles. Carlson treats these as a kind of "mnemonic architecture," where the layout of a site, the angles of its sightlines, and the dimensions of its stones preserve vital information across millennia.

To him, the ancients were not primitive people groping toward religion. They were survivors, or descendants of survivors, of the last reset. They understood that the sky was both clock and calendar, and that when certain patterns appeared overhead, the clock was counting down to upheaval. By encoding this knowledge into their most durable monuments, they ensured that the message could survive even if the language, culture, and political systems around it collapsed. In The Adam and Eve Story, Thomas describes the next cataclysm as something that could arrive with little warning to the unprepared, but with signs visible to those who knew where to look. Carlson's synthesis of planetary cycles, ancient sky maps, and sacred geometry makes that warning system tangible. It suggests that the last civilization didn't just try to warn us in myth, they left us instruments to measure the approach of the same forces that destroyed them.

This perspective also reframes the question of why the CIA or other agencies might suppress such information. If the patterns are real, and the timing can be predicted within decades or centuries, then the advantage lies with those who know first and prepare quietly. Public awareness would demand public infrastructure, resource distribution, and possibly even mass migrations, logistical nightmares that no ruling elite wants to manage. Far easier to let the knowledge decay into "mysticism" and "mythology," where it can be dismissed, while the initiated read the old instruments and plan accordingly.

By integrating sacred geometry with modern planetary science, Carlson bridges worlds, the empirical and the symbolic, the ancient and the modern. It's a bridge Thomas himself might have walked if he'd had access to the data we have now. And it's one more reminder that the full truth of Earth's cycles and the events that punctuate them is not hidden because it's unknowable, but because knowing it changes the stakes for everyone.

Carlson's work lives in the space between two camps that, for decades, spoke past each other. On one side is Charles Hapgood, with his model of sudden crust displacement, the Earth's outer shell slipping over its molten interior, dragging continents into new latitudes almost overnight. On the other is the growing body of modern impact theory, pointing to asteroid or comet strikes as the triggers for rapid climate change, extinctions, and geologic upheaval.

This is not idle speculation. Carlson shows how the timing of the Younger Dryas onset, around 12,800 years ago, lines up perfectly with the megaflood evidence, the nanodiamonds and meltglass found by the Comet Research Group, and the sudden climatic whiplash seen in ice cores. It's a moment in the geological record where the sky and the Earth seem to have conspired in catastrophe: something struck, something melted, and something shifted.

By synthesizing these lines of evidence, Carlson effectively updates Hapgood's theory for the modern era. Where Hapgood had to rely on historical cartography, anecdotal temperature shifts, and circumstantial fossil evidence, Carlson has access to high-resolution LiDAR maps, radiocarbon dating, and microphysical impact markers. The broad strokes are the same, sudden planetary reconfiguration, but the triggering mechanism is now clearer, and the evidence harder to dismiss.

This synthesis also changes the stakes of the conversation. If crust displacement is purely an internal Earth process, then perhaps it follows its own slow, unpredictable rhythm. But if it can be triggered by an external event, a cosmic impact, a solar outburst, or both, then it becomes a target for prediction. It means that the same planetary cycle work, the same ancient sky-watching traditions, and the same astronomical alignments Carlson studies could give us forewarning not just of impacts, but of the Earth's own response to them.

In this way, Carlson's bridge between Hapgood and modern impact science mirrors the bridge between Thomas's Adam and Eve Story and today's research. The old theories are not being replaced, they're being fortified. The picture is no longer a rough sketch. It's a layered, cross-checked map of how the Earth resets itself, and how often it might do so. And it's this map, more than any single paper or artifact, that makes the question of suppression so relevant.

The Younger Dryas
Smoking Gun

If you look at the climate record not as a gentle curve but as a seismograph, there is one point in recent geological history where the needle spikes like a heart under sudden shock. It is called the Younger Dryas onset, and it happened roughly 12,800 years ago. In an eyeblink of geological time, the planet plunged from a warming trend into an icehouse climate, glaciers re-advanced, ecosystems collapsed, and species that had survived for millions of years, the mammoth, the mastodon, the saber-toothed cat, vanished from the fossil record. It was a planetary trauma, a wound that scarred continents, cultures, and the memory of our species.

For decades, this transition was treated as a riddle wrapped in the language of "abrupt climate change," a phrase designed to name the phenomenon without naming the cause. The standard model mumbled about shifts in ocean currents or "meltwater pulses" as if those pulses were uncaused events that just happened to occur everywhere at once. What the textbooks left out was the possibility that this wasn't an internal hiccup in the Earth's system at all , but the fingerprint of something from above.

The Comet Research Group (CRG) is not the only team to look at that fingerprint, but they are the ones who have followed it with the tenacity of homicide detectives who know the suspect is still at large.

The case they've built is not based on vague correlations or speculative alignments. It's built on physical evidence in the dirt, evidence that can be picked up, measured, burned, and weighed. It is evidence that repeats itself across continents, locked in a thin layer of sediment like a chalk line marking the body.

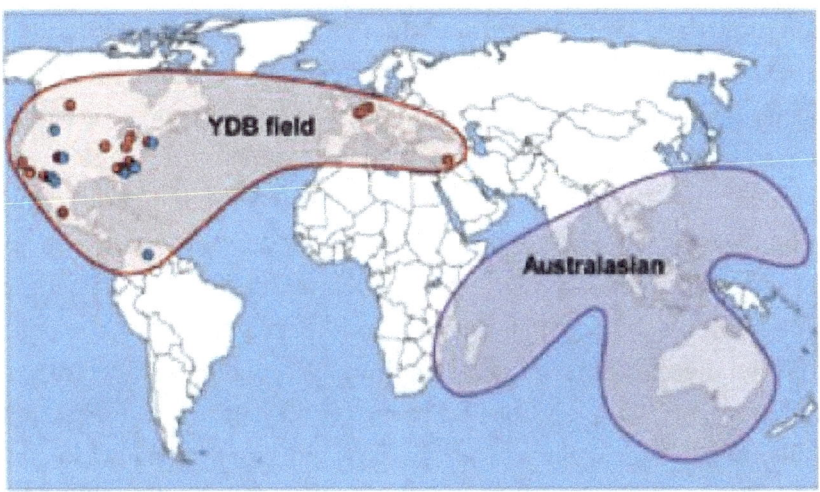

That layer, the Younger Dryas Boundary (YDB) , is the geological crime scene. In it, CRG scientists have found nanodiamonds: microscopic crystals of carbon that form under extreme heat and pressure, the kind generated in the heart of explosions or impacts so violent they vaporize rock. They've found microspherules, tiny glass beads formed when soil and stone are flash-melted into liquid and then rain back to Earth in droplets before cooling in midair. They've found meltglass, fused into bizarre shapes, sometimes containing minerals that can only form at temperatures hotter than volcanic lava, temperatures achievable by an asteroid strike or a cometary airburst. And they've found high concentrations of platinum, rare in Earth's crust but abundant in certain classes of meteorites.

These markers are not scattered randomly. They appear together, in the same order, at the same depth, all over the world: in North America, South America, Europe, the Middle East. They're locked into the same moment in time, confirmed by radiocarbon dating and stratigraphic analysis. You can dig them up in South Carolina, in Alberta, in Belgium, and in Syria, and the signature will be the same.

The implications are staggering. You don't get identical impact markers across multiple continents from local volcanic eruptions. You don't get them from lightning strikes or brush fires. You get them from something big enough and fast enough to affect the whole planet in the same geological instant. The CRG's conclusion: a fragmenting comet or asteroid, likely from the Taurid meteor complex, slammed into Earth's atmosphere and ice sheets around 12,800 years ago, releasing the energy of multiple nuclear arsenals, igniting massive wildfires, and throwing enough debris into the stratosphere to plunge the planet into a thousand-year deep freeze.

The climate shock fits. Ice core data from Greenland shows a temperature drop of 10 degrees Celsius in a matter of years, not centuries, not millennia, but years. This is not the slow work of drifting ocean currents. This is the kind of shift you get when sunlight is blotted out and heat balance is violently altered. Soot layers in those same ice cores match the timing of the YDB, pointing to continent-scale wildfires, the kind you'd expect if forests and grasslands across multiple continents ignited almost simultaneously under a rain of incandescent debris.

The ecological fallout was catastrophic. In North America alone, more than 30 species of megafauna disappeared forever, their extinction dates clustering at the Younger Dryas onset. The Clovis culture, the most widespread and sophisticated stone tool tradition on the continent, vanished from the archaeological record at the same time. Populations collapsed, survivors migrated or retreated into refugia, and the genetic bottlenecks visible in modern human DNA may have their roots in this exact disaster.

Mainstream science resisted this conclusion with a kind of bureaucratic fury, because it threatened too many comfortable narratives.

Catastrophism has always been the black sheep of geology, shunned in favor of gradualism, the slow and safe notion that the world changes in tiny increments. The CRG's data didn't fit that script. It suggested that Earth could be, and had been, blindsided by events far outside the control of climate models, carbon reduction plans, or human politics. It suggested that history itself might be punctuated by resets so sudden that entire civilizations could be erased in a single season.

Some of the resistance was methodological, critics nitpicked sampling procedures, lab contamination, or statistical treatment. But over the years, site after site confirmed the same markers, often by independent teams. The platinum anomaly alone, a spike in concentrations precisely at the YDB layer, has been replicated on multiple continents. The nanodiamonds, once contested, have now been found in such abundance at multiple sites that denying them borders on denialism. The meltglass compositions, the microspherule morphologies, the charcoal peaks, they all line up.

If you step back from the forensic detail and look at the broader implications, the CRG's work bridges directly to the cataclysmic triggers described by Charles Hapgood and echoed in Thomas's Adam and Eve Story. Hapgood imagined sudden crustal displacement as an internally-driven mechanism, but he acknowledged that such a shift could be triggered by external forces. What better trigger than the sudden removal of billions of tons of ice from one hemisphere, or the seismic shock of an impact? If a fragmenting comet hit the Laurentide ice sheet, the rapid melting and flooding could redistribute ocean mass and stress the crust in ways we are only beginning to model.

This is where the ancient record starts to matter. Because if such an event happened within the memory of early humans, the myths they passed down, of fire in the sky, of floods that swallowed the world, of darkness that lasted for years, cease to be purely metaphorical. The flood of the Sumerians, the fire serpents of the Americas, the "gods" descending in blazing chariots, these could be the cultural memories of the Younger Dryas impact. And those memories were not just stories. They were warnings.

What CRG has made clear is that this was not a one-off freak oc-
currence. We live in a cosmic shooting gallery. The Taurid meteor
complex, a sprawling stream of debris from a giant comet that broke
apart tens of thousands of years ago, still intersects Earth's orbit twice
a year. Astronomers have identified large, still-dangerous objects
within it, some of them potentially capable of delivering the same
kind of blow that ended the Pleistocene. Every June and November,
we pass through that debris stream. Most of it is harmless dust, burning up as meteors. But not all of it is dust.

The uncomfortable truth is that the probability of another Younger
Dryas-scale impact within the next few millennia is not negligible.
In cosmic terms, it is inevitable. And here is where the CRG's work
brushes against the same wall of silence that seems to have met
Thomas's manuscript in the 1960s. Acknowledging the real risk
means acknowledging that we are not in control, that our infrastructure and supply chains and fragile global systems could be shredded
in a matter of days. It means that survival would favor the prepared,
those with access to deep shelters, independent resources, and prior
warning. And that is knowledge the modern equivalent of the old
priesthood may prefer to keep to themselves.

The Younger Dryas boundary layer is not speculation. You can hold it
in your hands. You can crush the sediment and see the tiny glass beads
glint in the sunlight. You can send it to a lab and watch the instruments register carbon forms that only exist when matter has been to
hell and back. And yet, outside of a few circles, the public has no idea
it exists. That is not an accident.

The Comet Research Group has, in effect, given us the smoking gun
of planetary catastrophe, a weapon still loaded, still pointed, and still
in the room. The question is not whether it will fire again, but when,
and whether we will see the muzzle flash in time to do anything about
it. Thomas suspected the trigger. Hapgood mapped the motion. CRG
has found the bullet hole. The rest of the picture, the body on the

floor, the motive, the next victim, is for us to piece together before the next round is chambered.

Graham Hancock – The Historian of Forgotten Worlds

If the Comet Research Group provides the forensic evidence of catastrophe, Graham Hancock has spent his career assembling the cultural testimony. His archive is not stored in a lab freezer or sediment core repository, it's scattered across myths, megaliths, and forbidden archaeology sites that official history would rather not discuss. Where the scientists sift milligrams of boundary sediment for nanodiamonds, Hancock sifts entire civilizations for clues they left behind about a world that came before.

From the moment Fingerprints of the Gods hit shelves in 1995, Hancock's central claim has been a thorn in the side of mainstream archaeology: that a highly capable civilization , not "primitive" hunter-gatherers , existed before the end of the last Ice Age, and that it was destroyed in a global cataclysm. The survivors, he argues, became the seed-bearers of civilization, passing fragments of their knowledge to later cultures, who enshrined it in stone, myth, and ritual.

His journeys have taken him from the high Andes to the floor of the Indian Ocean, from Angkor Wat to the Great Sphinx. In each case, the story is similar: impossibly precise architecture that defies the assumed technological limits of its builders, alignments to celestial events thousands of years in the past, and oral traditions that speak of floods, fire from the sky, and an age of darkness. Hancock's books read like travelogues through the memory of the human race, always circling back to the idea that we are a species with amnesia.

For decades, critics dismissed him as a romantic or conspiracy theorist. But the emergence of the Younger Dryas Impact Hypothesis, with its smoking-gun sediment layers and global distribution of cosmic markers, has shifted the ground beneath his detractors. Suddenly, the central event in Hancock's narrative, a sudden, civilization-wiping disaster at the end of the Ice Age, has hard scientific evidence behind it. The Comet Research Group's fieldwork has, in a sense, validated the catastrophe Hancock has been pointing to for 30 years.

But Hancock is not satisfied with proving a disaster happened. His deeper question is: how did those who survived try to warn the future? If your world was erased, and you knew the sky could erase it again, how would you leave a message that might survive 10,000 years of forgetfulness, linguistic drift, and social collapse? His answer, and the answer of many ancient cultures, is to encode that message in stone, in ways that resist both erosion and censorship.

Which brings the trail inexorably to southeastern Turkey, and to the most paradigm-shattering archaeological site ever discovered: Göbekli Tepe. This is not just another entry in Hancock's atlas of anomalies. It is the crown jewel , the "smoking temple" to match the "smoking gun" of the Younger Dryas Boundary.

When Hancock visited Göbekli Tepe, he saw not just the artistry of its T-shaped pillars and animal carvings, but the timeline: it was built before agriculture, before cities, before the official start of "civilization" as we define it. The conventional model says that culture grows from farming. Göbekli Tepe suggests that farming may have been a survival adaptation, a way for people who had just lived through the end of the world to rebuild enough stability to support monumental construction.

For Hancock, the correlation with the end of the Younger Dryas is not

an accident. The same cataclysm the Comet Research Group has identified as an impact event may have been the very disaster that ended
the previous civilization and triggered the building of Göbekli Tepe.
Its pillars could be more than ritual markers, they could be a coded
star map, a record of the sky as it appeared during the catastrophe, left
behind as both a memorial and a warning.

In this light, Göbekli Tepe is not just an archaeological marvel, it
is the bridge between physical evidence and cultural memory. It is
where Hancock's thesis and the CRG's data meet in solid, immovable
limestone. And it is here, on this hill in Turkey, that the story turns
from the realm of sediment and stone into one of symbols and inten-
tional design, a chapter written for the future by those who had just
survived the past.

Göbekli Tepe – The Message in Stone

The hill rises modestly over the plains of southeastern Turkey, but what lies beneath it has detonated the carefully curated narrative of human history. Until the 1990s, our official timeline was tidy: agriculture led to villages, villages to cities, and cities to temples. Civilization was the byproduct of farming, which itself could only emerge after the Ice Age's grip loosened. That's the story we were taught, steady, linear, predictable. Göbekli Tepe blew that story open.

Copyright DAI, Gobekli Tepe Project

Under the soil lay concentric stone circles, each built from massive T-shaped pillars up to 18 feet tall and weighing as much as 15 tons. The pillars were carved from limestone with an artistry and precision that should have been far beyond the reach of so-called "primitive" hunter-gatherers. The surfaces bear intricate reliefs of animals, foxes, snakes, cranes, scorpions, wild boar, along with abstract symbols and stylized human forms. The complexity of the art and engineering alone is staggering.

But the real shock comes from the dates. Radiocarbon testing of organic material embedded in the fill puts the earliest phases of Göbekli Tepe at around 9600 BCE. That's more than 7,000 years before Stonehenge and nearly as long before the pyramids of Giza. According to our textbooks, people of that era were nomadic, living in small bands, struggling daily for survival. Yet here was proof that someone, perhaps many someones , had both the resources and the organizational skill to quarry, transport, and erect multi-ton megaliths in carefully planned arrangements.

This raises the question: was Göbekli Tepe the start of civilization, or the end of something much older? The timing lines up with almost suspicious precision: the end of the Younger Dryas cold snap, the same moment the Comet Research Group identifies as the aftermath of a planet-altering impact. If that cataclysm erased an earlier, advanced culture, Göbekli Tepe may have been built by its survivors, not as a beginning, but as an attempt to preserve what they knew.

The very act of monumental building suggests a purpose beyond the mundane. You don't carve and haul stones this size to honor the harvest if you don't yet have one. You do it to send a message, to mark a place, to fix something in time and space so it cannot be forgotten. The layout of the enclosures, the placement of the pillars, and the careful carving of specific animals and symbols hint at a language of stone, one we are only beginning to decode.

Even more mysterious is the deliberate burial. After centuries of use, the builders, or their descendants, backfilled the enclosures with tons of debris, sealing them off from the world. This wasn't collapse or neglect. It was purposeful, systematic, and thorough, as though they wanted the site preserved for a distant future they would never see.

Was it to protect sacred knowledge? To hide a warning from those not ready, or not worthy, to understand it? Or was the meaning already lost, and the burial simply an act of closure by people who no longer grasped what their ancestors had intended? We cannot say. But we can note the uncanny fact that this site, with its precision carvings and its astronomical hints, lay hidden until the late 20th century, exactly the moment when we are rediscovering the very cataclysm it may have been built to memorialize.

Pillar 43 — The Sky Map of a Disaster

The so-called "Vulture Stone" (Pillar 43) is a slab of carved warnings wrapped in astronomical code. At first glance: a vulture with a sphere, a scorpion, other birds, strange shapes, and three "handbag" symbols floating above it all. To most archaeologists, these are ritual images. To those willing to align the carvings with ancient skies, they are a precise map of constellations.

The vulture likely represents Cygnus. In ancient sky lore, this is a key reference point near the North Celestial Pole, critical for navigation and timekeeping.

The scorpion is unmistakably Scorpius, a constellation tied to danger and death in myth. Its position in the carving matches where it would have appeared during a major cataclysm window around 14,800 BCE.

Göbekli Tepe - Pillar 43: Animal Carvings to Proposed Constellations

Animal Carving	Proposed Constellation(s) / Symbolism
Scorpion	Scorpius
Vulture	Sagittarius / Cygnus
Crane + adjacent bird	Ophiuchus / Pisces
Dog / Wolf	Lupus / Aquarius
Ibex / Quadruped	Gemini
Frog / Small creature	Virgo / Bear
Sun/moon disks / V-symbols	Calendar markers
Headless man / Geometric	Soul transition / Mythic

The sphere the vulture holds may mark the Sun or a significant celestial body at a precise point in the precession cycle, a date stamp in stone.

The three "handbags", so often dismissed as decorative, could be schematic survival markers. In the ECDO model, a crust shift would send ocean water flooding inland, swallowing lowlands for decades or centuries. Safe zones would be elevated plateaus or hills. In this reading, each "handbag" is a depiction of such a high refuge, Göbekli Tepe itself, Karahan Tepe nearby, and perhaps a third site like Sayburç.

Other carvings suggest sky phenomena consistent with a crust shift: wavy lines that could represent aurora borealis seen far south of normal, or shockwave patterns from a catastrophic atmosphere–ocean interaction.

The Decoded Warning

Put together, Pillar 43 reads less like "sacred art" and more like a briefing slide:

Here is the sky when the last disaster came.

Here are the safe zones.

Here is what will happen

Flood, fire, cold.

And then, the site was buried. Possibly because the survivors feared looters, or worse, feared that knowing too much might hasten the next disaster.

The Burial and the Pause – Why the Dig Stopped

If the stones of Göbekli Tepe were meant to survive millennia, they have succeeded. But our window into their full meaning may be narrowing. In recent years, excavation at the site has slowed dramatically, and some areas have been deliberately left unexcavated. Official explanations cite the need for preservation, the dangers of exposing fragile carvings to the elements, and the importance of developing better conservation techniques.

These reasons are valid , ancient limestone is vulnerable once uncovered , but for those inclined toward suspicion, the halt raises questions. Göbekli Tepe is not just a scientific curiosity; it's a potential rewrite of human history. If certain findings might support "unapproved" narratives, such as the existence of an advanced pre-agricultural civilization or a direct link to cosmic cataclysms , would they be made public immediately? Or would they be managed, trickled out, or quietly buried again?

We've seen similar patterns before: anomalous finds locked away in museum basements, inconvenient data sidelined in journals, sites left unexplored because their implications are too disruptive. Göbekli Tepe, with its impossible age, its deliberate burial, and its carved symbols that seem to map the heavens, sits at the center of this tension.

Perhaps the archaeologists are simply doing their best under difficult circumstances. Or perhaps, as with Thomas's Adam and Eve Story, there are those who believe that some truths are too destabilizing for general release. Either way, the stones will keep their secrets a while longer. But they will not keep them forever.

The Boneyards of the North

In the frozen north, far beyond the reach of summer's warmth, there are places where the Earth holds memories it would rather keep buried. Alaska, the Yukon, and across to Siberia, the land itself has become an archive of catastrophe. Beneath layers of permafrost and ancient muck lie tangled masses of bone, graveyards that defy the patience of slow geological time. These aren't quiet burials from a gradual winnowing of life. They are chaotic, violent deposits, a jumble of creatures from different worlds, pressed together in death.

When the first gold miners arrived in the Klondike in the late 19th century, they weren't expecting to become accidental paleontologists. Hydraulic hoses tore into frozen riverbanks, blasting away walls of silt and gravel. Out spilled mammoth tusks, bison skulls, camels' teeth, and horse bones, some still streaked with reddish flesh and sinew. The miners told of dogs chewing the meat as if it had been preserved only a few seasons, not for tens of thousands of years. For scientists trained to think in terms of gradual extinction, these reports were inconvenient. They were filed away, footnotes in mining journals, while the gold rush stories focused on fortunes found in metal, not the remains of an Arctic Eden.

The jumbled deposits made little sense in the framework of slow-moving glaciers. Lions, mastodons, and antelope, creatures that would never have shared the same range, were found piled together. Some bones were shattered and splintered, not by the slow crush of ice but as if tossed in a violent current and dashed against stone. In certain deposits, entire skeletons lay in twisted, unnatural positions, necks bent back, legs folded under as if the animal had been knocked from its feet mid-stride.

The Berezovka Mammoth, discovered in Siberia in 1901, was one of the most famous of these frozen relics. Found standing upright in the ice, its flesh so well-preserved that it gave off the smell of decaying meat, it still had buttercups in its mouth and undigested plants in its stomach. For some, this was an open-and-shut case of sudden freezing, a living creature caught in the middle of grazing, instantly entombed. The official explanation settled on "a fall into a crevasse," but that neat answer failed to account for the hundreds of similar finds across the high latitudes.

Farther east, in the Yukon's Bluefish Caves, layers of bone tell a similar story, not of a slow accumulation, but of sudden surges. The deposits show evidence of massive flooding, with the remains of predators and prey alike swept together and buried in the same strata. Elsewhere in Alaska, caves have yielded bison skulls alongside the bones of marine mammals, suggesting that ocean waters, pushed far inland, may have reached these remote chambers. The mixture of species is the signature of a disaster that cared nothing for ecological boundaries.

Charles Hapgood, with his controversial theory of rapid crustal displacement, saw these northern boneyards as key evidence. If the poles shifted rapidly, a region that was once temperate could be plunged into the deep freeze in days or even hours. The animals grazing on open grasslands would be overtaken by a wall of wind and ice, swept into rivers turned to torrents, and frozen before decay could begin. His detractors dismissed this as fanciful, but the image of a mammoth with fresh plants in its mouth has never fully left the public imagination.

Today, most scientists explain these finds with the slower tools of climate change, overhunting, and gradual ice advance. Yet these explanations stumble when confronted with the sheer violence written into the fossil record. Mass death deposits in Alaska's Fairbanks Creek or Siberia's Yana River delta show not just cold, but chaos, bones broken, crushed, and scattered as if by a force far beyond winter's creeping reach.

To walk these sites today is to feel the unease of a land that remembers more than it will tell. The permafrost hides its story well, but now and then a thaw or a mining operation tears open the archive, and for a moment, the past rushes out, the smell of ancient flesh, the gleam of ivory, the curve of a horn that has not seen daylight in an age. These are the testimonies that remain when the myths fade and the monuments crumble.

The people who have lived in these northern lands for millennia tell of sudden cold, of great floods that came without warning, of animals and humans alike swept away. Their oral histories speak of worlds overturned, of hunting grounds lost under ice in a single season. Whether or not one accepts Hapgood's rapid pole shift or The Ethical Skeptic's exothermic core-mantle decoupling, the bones themselves are there, locked in the ground, daring us to explain them.

In these boneyards, science and legend meet in uneasy truce. We can measure the isotopes, date the layers, and model the climate shifts, but the deeper truth may be written not in numbers but in the quiet, stubborn presence of the remains themselves, silent witnesses to a day when something vast and sudden came for the living world, and did not stop until it had remade the face of the Earth.

Ben Davidson – The Solar Killshot

If comet impacts are the sniper's bullet from deep space, then the solar micronova is the shotgun blast from across the table. Both can erase civilizations in a geological instant, but the micronova has a crueler twist: it doesn't need to travel millions of miles. It starts at home, in the heart of the star that sustains us. Ben Davidson has spent the last decade tracking the signs that this shotgun may already be cocked. Davidson, founder of the SuspiciousObservers research collective, is not a credentialed astrophysicist by the conventional yardstick, but like Hancock in archaeology, he has built a following by making connections that mainstream gatekeepers either can't see or won't acknowledge. His daily briefings on solar activity, magnetic field behavior, and space weather pull from peer-reviewed sources and satellite data, but the synthesis is his own. The picture he paints is not one of slow, stable stellar output. It is one of a star that occasionally, and catastrophically, loses its temper.

The micronova hypothesis is simple in its horror. The Sun, under certain conditions, can store massive amounts of energy in its magnetic fields. When those fields become unstable, whether through internal cycles, galactic influences, or interactions with Earth's own magnetic field, the stored energy can be released in a single, violent outburst. Not a steady coronal mass ejection (CME) of the type we've seen in the space age, but a superflare orders of magnitude more powerful.

Evidence for such events is not confined to theory. Ice cores from Greenland and Antarctica bear chemical signatures, sudden spikes in isotopes like beryllium-10 and carbon-14, that indicate enormous surges of cosmic radiation striking Earth in the recent geological past. Tree rings show similar anomalies. Some of these spikes correspond to known solar events, like the 774–775 CE "Miyake Event," which caused a dramatic jump in atmospheric radiocarbon. But Davidson points to even larger, more dangerous spikes in the deeper past, events that could only be explained by a solar outburst dwarfing anything recorded in human history.

In Davidson's model, a micronova could be triggered or amplified during a geomagnetic excursion, a temporary but extreme weakening of Earth's magnetic field. The field acts as a shield, deflecting much of the solar wind and radiation. If that shield collapses or thins dramatically, as it has many times in the past, even a smaller-than-average solar eruption could deliver extinction-level effects on the surface.

And that, he argues, is exactly the situation we are sliding into now. Measurements from satellites like ESA's Swarm mission show that Earth's magnetic field has been weakening at an accelerating pace for at least 150 years, with some regions, particularly the South Atlantic Anomaly, deteriorating far faster. The magnetic poles are also migrating at unprecedented speeds. In Davidson's view, this is the prelude to a full-blown excursion, an event that tends to occur on cycles of roughly 12,000 years. The last one? Right around the end of the Younger Dryas.

The overlap is unsettling. Hapgood's crustal displacement theory, once sidelined by the gradualist orthodoxy, may find new relevance here. A geomagnetic excursion is not just an electromagnetic problem; it could destabilize the rotational balance of Earth's crust and mantle. Combine that with the gravitational and magnetic chaos of a micronova event, and you have a recipe for rapid, catastrophic change, the kind of "instant shift" hinted at in both ancient myth and suppressed scientific whispers.

Davidson does not stop at theory. He points to planetary evidence: Mars, stripped of much of its atmosphere, bearing clear scars of massive electrical discharges; the Moon's glassy spherules and vitrified soil; even Mercury's pockmarked surface, which he suggests may record solar outbursts from long before the inner planets settled into their current orbits. These are the crime scenes of the inner solar system, and they suggest the killer lives next door.

The human consequences of such an event are difficult to overstate. A sufficiently large micronova could ignite global wildfires, flash-melt ice sheets, vaporize coastal cities with instant steam surges, and plunge surviving populations into centuries of unstable climate. Even a weaker version, timed with a geomagnetic collapse, could wipe out satellites, electrical grids, and all modern communications in hours, a technological amputation from which there is no quick recovery.

Davidson's work also ties directly into elite preparation narratives. If you knew such a cycle was real, and you had the resources to act, you wouldn't just build underground bunkers for nuclear war. You'd build them deep enough, shielded enough, and stocked enough to survive years without sunlight, in case the Sun itself became the enemy. You'd map the safest latitudes, the most stable crustal blocks, and the aquifers least likely to be contaminated by fallout or saltwater intrusion. You'd seed survival knowledge into cultural projects that could outlast a collapse.

Sound familiar? It's the same logic we saw with the Comet Research Group's catastrophe; the same long-term warning impulse Hancock reads into Göbekli Tepe. The only difference is the trigger, rock from space versus fire from our own star. In truth, these are not separate threats. They are entangled. A geomagnetic collapse could make us vulnerable to both at once. A comet impact could destabilize the Sun's activity. The cycles that govern one may well govern the other.

Davidson's critics accuse him of alarmism. But they rarely dispute the underlying data: the field is weakening, the poles are moving, the historical record contains spikes in cosmic radiation we cannot fully explain, and other stars have been observed to nova on small, cyclical scales. They focus instead on whether these patterns will converge in our lifetime. Davidson's answer is not comforting: "Soon enough that you should be ready."

In the context of the Adam and Eve narrative, Davidson's solar micronova hypothesis is not a replacement for Hapgood's crustal shift or the Younger Dryas impact. It is the missing amplifier. It is the force that could take a marginally survivable event and push it over the edge into extinction-level territory. It may even be the clock driving the whole cycle, a 6000-year heartbeat of destruction and renewal, carved into the rhythms of both Earth and Sun.

And if that is true, then the message carved into stone by the survivors of the last cycle is not just about rocks from the sky. It's about the sky itself turning on us. The foxes, vultures, and scorpions on Göbekli Tepe's pillars may not just be constellations, they may be a bestiary of death, a symbolic record of all the ways the heavens can kill. The burial of the site may have been a ritual goodbye to a stable world they knew would not last.

Davidson's warning is blunt: watch the Sun. Watch the field. Watch the sky. If all three begin to move in dangerous sync, the countdown has already started.

The Ethical Skeptic - ECDO Theory

If Hapgood's crustal displacement is the opening act, and Chan Thomas's "Adam and Eve" story is the bootlegged blueprint, then The Ethical Skeptic's ECDO theory is the black box recording, a post-incident analysis telling us not only what happened, but why it will happen again. It doesn't rely on just one domain of evidence. It stitches together climate anomalies, archaeology, magnetic field data, mechanical physics, and the language of ancient myth into a single, unnerving cycle. And it points squarely at the Earth's own heart, the nickel-iron core, as both the engine of life and the fuse for global catastrophe.

We've been told to think of climate change as a story of human carbon output and melting ice caps. But ECDO forces a different perspective: what if the heat isn't coming from above at all? What if it comes from below? Imagine the core, under immense pressure, shifting its lattice structure, like a compressed spring suddenly snapping into a new position, and in that process releasing stored kinetic energy as heat. That heat rises through the mantle, through the asthenosphere, into the deep oceans first, altering currents, destabilizing methane hydrates, and warping climate patterns in ways that make the last century's CO_2 debate look like a magician's misdirection.

This is not an abstract guess. The oceans are heating from the bottom.

2023 saw abyssal temperatures spike beyond climate model projections, with deep methane releases outpacing every IPCC forecast. And, almost as if on cue, Earth's geomagnetic field has been in accelerated decline for the last 150 years, shedding about 10% of its strength per century, a process that may be directly tied to the changes in the core ECDO describes.

But the core–mantle dynamic isn't just a climate story. It's a rotation story. Here's where the Dzhanibekov effect, the unnerving flip you can watch in any physics lab, becomes more than a party trick. In that effect, a rigid body in free rotation with a shifting internal mass distribution can suddenly snap into a new orientation. According to ECDO, the Earth is essentially a gyroscope with two competing modes of rotational stability: magnetic-moment equilibrium and inertial-moment equilibrium. For most of its cycle, the strong geomagnetic core locks the outer layers into a magnetic-moment priority, stable, predictable, safe. But in the decoupling phase, when the magnetic moment collapses, the outer shell, mantle and crust, is free to seek inertial balance. And when it does, the axis moves.

Not a slow, graceful drift over tens of thousands of years. A shift. Sudden enough to be recorded in myth as "the day the Sun stood still" or "the night that lasted three days." Violent enough to drive ocean waters hundreds of feet above current sea level, leaving karst erosion bands on the upper tiers of the Khafre Pyramid , the kind of "dead body" evidence that can't be waved away with academic hand-waving. Those bands tell a simple, devastating story: the Giza Plateau was under ocean water for decades, maybe centuries, at a stable elevation hundreds of feet higher than today's seas. No storm surge, no river flood can explain it. Only a rebalanced planet, its crust and oceans redistributed by a rotational shock, could.

This isn't a fringe reading of a single ruin. The same cycle is etched into monuments, artifacts, and oral traditions worldwide. Over 175 distinct cultures have "flood myths," many of them paired with celestial upheaval, strange skies, wandering stars, pillars of fire. These are not just campfire stories; they are memory capsules, passed through generations to warn us: "This happened before. It will happen again." According to ECDO, the geographic axis of rotation tends to move along the 31° East meridian during these flips, the same line that passes through both the Giza Plateau and the geographic center of the landmasses on Earth. That's not a random alignment. It's a fingerprint.

The trigger is a combination of mechanical and thermal effects. The exothermic shedding of material in the D" layer, the boundary zone between core and mantle, lubricates the shift. Once decoupled, the outer shell rotates into a new equilibrium, potentially swinging up to 104° from its current position. That's not just polar migration; that's a wholesale reconfiguration of climate zones, coastlines, and survivable latitudes in the space of a human lifetime.

The return to the magnetic-moment equilibrium takes longer. The cycle breathes. Civilizations rise in the long, quiet periods, forgetting the last breath out. Then the next decoupling begins, and the forgetting becomes fatal.

The Ethical Skeptic places us well past what he calls the Indigo Point, the threshold beyond which the heat and instability from the core are locked into the system. From here, the question is not whether the next Tau Point flip will happen, but when. And while he won't claim a precise date, the confluence of indicators, deep ocean warming, magnetic field collapse, polar acceleration, unexplained methane releases, suggests we're not centuries away.

Here's the cruel irony: the same institutions that lecture us about "following the science" have embargoed this line of inquiry for decades. Funding dries up. Careers vanish. Findings get buried in journals no one reads. And all the while, ancient stone records , from the erosion bands on Khafre to the astronomical alignments at Göbekli Tepe , sit in plain view, ignored or misrepresented.

The Ethical Skeptic closes his hypothesis with a line that could serve as the epitaph for modern civilization: "Man himself has proved to be a greater threat to our knowledge and understanding than any natural disaster ever could be." Our enemies are not only comets, micronovae, or core shifts. They are the priests of orthodoxy, whether wearing the robes of religion or the lab coats of "settled science", who burn the libraries, chisel out the inscriptions, and rebury the artifacts in the name of God or Science. Same team. Same playbook.

The Earth will turn again. The only question is whether we will face it as a species with amnesia, or as one that remembers.

Conclusion — The Forgotten Pattern

From the moment the CIA clipped The Adam and Eve Story down to a thin pamphlet, the pattern was already clear. When knowledge threatens power, it is hidden. Not always destroyed, sometimes just buried, truncated, or locked in a vault under the banner of "national security." Chan Thomas may have been one of many who stumbled too close to the real trigger mechanism behind Earth's recurring resets, and the agency's redaction wasn't about copyright or classification law. It was about control.

Hapgood, under the polite cover of academic geography, poked at the same nerve. His first maps and theories hinted at a rapid, devastating crust shift, perhaps hours or days, not millennia, but later works softened the blow, as if the raw truth had been massaged into something less actionable. The threads of his early research still lead north to expeditions and whispers of a world turned sideways in an instant.

The Ethical Skeptic's ECDO theory revives the mechanical heart of this catastrophe cycle: a decoupling between core and mantle, lubricated by exothermic release, allowing the outer shell to shift violently over the interior. The scars are there, in the erosion bands of the Khafre Pyramid, in the megaflood landscapes Randall Carlson has spent decades mapping, in the deep-time sky maps carved into ancient stone.

Graham Hancock's "lost civilization" is no fantasy romance for archaeologists to mock. It's the missing witness. The people who saw the last shift survived it and set about building a message that could cross thousands of years. Göbekli Tepe, and especially Pillar 43, is not primitive art, it's a disaster log. A constellational clock. A survival map for the next time the Earth jerks on its axis.

We have spent fifty years since Chan Thomas's redaction filling in the missing pieces, from ice-core climate spikes to platinum-rich Younger Dryas layers, from buried megalithic complexes to the open suppression of excavation. The puzzle is no longer about whether a reset comes, but when. And whether, when the signs line up again, we will recognize them, or dismiss them as quaint myth, just as most of our own scientists now do.

If this knowledge has always been the province of a few, pharaohs, priests, emperors, kings, presidents, then we are faced with an uncomfortable truth. The last civilization may have died trying to warn us, but our own elites seem more interested in surviving quietly than in sharing the map. The DUMBs, the seed vaults, the silent engineering projects under mountains, these are not made for you.

That leaves the burden with us, the uninvited. We are not building Göbekli Tepes, but we can record, disseminate, and preserve what we know. We can resist the reflex to scoff at "myth" and instead test it against geology, astronomy, and archaeology. And above all, we can refuse to let this warning be buried again.

Because when the sky tilts and the seas climb, it will not matter how many hashtags we posted, how many panel discussions we held, or how many degrees we earned. It will matter only whether we understood the pattern, and whether we acted on it in time.

When the Earth shifts again, whether by the slow grinding of time or in a single violent snap, there will be no more warnings, no more debates, no more second chances. The monuments, the myths, the redacted pages, and the buried stones all told us the same thing: this has happened before, and it will happen again. The only question left is whether we will face it as the last civilization did, scrambling in the dark, leaving a tomb of warnings for strangers, or whether we will finally break the cycle and meet the next dawn with our eyes wide open.

Bibliography and References

Primary Historical & Scientific Sources

Hapgood, Charles H. Earth's Shifting Crust. New York: Pantheon Books, 1958.

https://archive.org/details/earthsshiftingcrust

Hapgood, Charles H. Path of the Pole. New York: Chilton Company, 1970.

https://archive.org/details/path-of-the-pole

Thomas, Chan. The Adam and Eve Story: The History of Cataclysms. CIA Declassified Version, 1993.

https://www.cia.gov/readingroom/document/cia-rdp79b00752a000300070001-8

Einstein, Albert. "Foreword" in Earth's Shifting Crust, by Charles H. Hapgood. New York: Pantheon, 1958.

Velikovsky, Immanuel. Worlds in Collision. New York: Macmillan, 1950.

https://archive.org/details/worldsincollision00veli

Modern Cataclysm Research

Carlson, Randall. "Cataclysms and the Cycle of Ages." Kosmographia Podcast, Episode 22, February 2020.

https://www.youtube.com/@RandallCarlson

Carlson, Randall. "Megafloods and the Younger Dryas Impact Hypothesis." Lecture, 2019.
https://www.youtube.com/watch?v=G0Cp7DrvNLQ

Comet Research Group. "Younger Dryas Impact Hypothesis Research Papers."
https://cometresearchgroup.org/

Hancock, Graham. Fingerprints of the Gods. London: Heinemann, 1995.
https://grahamhancock.com/fotg/

Hancock, Graham. Magicians of the Gods. London: Coronet, 2015.
https://grahamhancock.com/motg/

Hancock, Graham. America Before: The Key to Earth's Lost Civilization. London: Coronet, 2019.
https://grahamhancock.com/america-before/

Davidson, Ben. The Next End of the World. SuspiciousObservers.org, 2022.
https://suspicious0bservers.org/

The Ethical Skeptic. "Exothermic Core-Mantle Decoupling – Dzhanibekov Oscillation Hypothesis." February 16, 2020.
https://theethicalskeptic.com/

Archaeology & Ancient Monuments

Schmidt, Klaus. Göbekli Tepe: A Stone Age Sanctuary in South-Eastern Anatolia. Berlin: Deutsches Archäologisches Institut, 2010.

Schoch, Robert M. "A New Look at Göbekli Tepe." Atlantis Rising Magazine, Issue 122, 2017.
https://www.robertschoch.com/

Magli, Giulio. Architecture, Astronomy and Sacred Landscape in Ancient Egypt. Cambridge University Press, 2013.

West, John Anthony. Serpent in the Sky: The High Wisdom of Ancient Egypt. Wheaton: Quest Books, 1993.

Mythology, History, and Cultural Accounts

Hamilton, Edith. Mythology: Timeless Tales of Gods and Heroes. New York: Little, Brown, and Company, 1942.

Frazer, James George. The Golden Bough. London: Macmillan, 1890.
https://archive.org/details/goldenboughstud00fraz

The Bible. Genesis 6–9, The Flood Narrative.

Epic of Gilgamesh. Translated by Andrew George. London: Penguin Classics, 1999.

Declassified & Government Documents

Central Intelligence Agency. "The Adam and Eve Story – Classified Copy." CIA-RDP79B00752A000300070001-8, 1993.
https://www.cia.gov/readingroom/document/cia-rdp79b00752a000300070001-8

U.S. Geological Survey. "Crustal Deformation and Plate Tectonics Research Reports."
https://www.usgs.gov/

www.ingramcontent.com/pod-product-compliance
Lightning Source LLC
Chambersburg PA
CBHW071206120626
46546CB00006B/2438